EVERY

MINUTE

IS A DAY

EVERY MINUTE IS A DAY

A DOCTOR, AN EMERGENCY ROOM,

and a CITY UNDER SIEGE

Robert Meyer, MD, *and* Dan Koeppel

CROWN

NEW YORK

Library of Congress Cataloging-in-Publication Data
Names: Meyer, Robert (Robert H.), author. |
Koeppel, Dan, author.
Title: Every minute is a day / Robert Meyer and Dan Koeppel.
Description: First edition. | New York: Crown, [2021]
Identifiers: LCCN 2021012301 (print) |
LCCN 2021012302 (ebook) | ISBN 9780593238592 (hardcover) |
ISBN 9780593238608 (ebook)
Subjects: LCSH: Meyer, Robert (Robert H.) | Montefiore Medical
Center. | COVID-19 Pandemic, 2020—-New York (State)—
New York. | COVID-19 (Disease)—Patients—New York (State)—
New York. | Emergency physicians—New York (State)—
New York—Anecdotes. | Hospitals—Emergency services—
New York (State)—New York.
Classification: LCC RA644.C67 M48 2021 (print) |
LCC RA644.C67 (ebook) | DDC 362.1962/41409747—dc23
LC record available at https://lccn.loc.gov/2021012301
LC ebook record available at https://lccn.loc.gov/2021012302

Printed in the United States of America on acid-free paper

crownpublishing.com

246897531

First Edition

During the Covid-19 pandemic, many, many people died alone, without their loved ones being able to see them or say goodbye. This book is dedicated to the survivors who are still feeling that loss and will always feel it. It is not an adequate substitute for being there, for holding a hand, for giving a final embrace, but we hope that they can find some small comfort in knowing that we tried our best to honor and respect those this disease claimed.

Keep a looking glass in your own heart, and the more carefully you scan your own frailties, the more tender you are for those of your fellow creatures.

—DR. WILLIAM OSLER, 1849–1919. CONSIDERED BY MANY TO BE THE FATHER OF MODERN, PATIENT-CENTERED MEDICINE. FROM *THE QUOTABLE OSLER*, 2008, THE AMERICAN COLLEGE OF PHYSICIANS.

Foreword

In the late winter of 2020, I was with my family in Portland, Maine. I began to understand what was at stake as Covid-19 spread when my employer at the time, *The New York Times,* shifted the entire staff to remote work. A few days later, the schools that my children attended closed to in-person instruction and care. I was worried about all the things everyone else was worried about: the health and well-being of my family, my family's productivity at work and school, helping others in my community. But I had one particular source of anxiety as I read about cases of Covid appearing in New York City, where I was born and raised.

For twenty-five years, my cousin Rob Meyer has been an emergency room doctor in the Bronx at Montefiore Medical Center, whose three associated hospitals and satellite clinics (which all together are officially referred to as the

Montefiore Health System), by some counts, treat more emergency room patients than any other facility in the United States. Rob is one of the most dedicated physicians I know. He cares about his patients not only when they're in medical need but throughout their lives. Rob was influenced by my late father, Richard Koeppel, who was also an ER doctor. And as a teaching physician at the Albert Einstein College of Medicine, Montefiore's affiliated educational institution, Rob has instructed hundreds of medical students. Rob has always met his obligations head-on, even when it has meant putting his own safety at risk.

So, as the pandemic began to take shape, I sent him a text message: *How are you doing? I'm worried for you.*

Hanging by a thread, Rob replied.

Are you seeing a lot of cases?

Yes.

On a scale of 1 to 10, where do you think you are?

The next reply took awhile—something I'm used to with Rob; it nearly always means he's handling a crisis. After ten minutes, I got an answer: *Do you really want to know?*

I did.

100.

That exchange opened the door to a series of texts from Rob that I found upsetting, tragic, and—to be honest— fascinating. Rob indicated that talking about what was happening was helpful to him, so I encouraged him to message, call, or send me voice memos—whatever he needed to do to help him cope.

I will, but don't tell my family. He made me promise. *I don't want them to worry.*

Rob's texts, emails, and confessional phone calls, as well as our in-person discussions, ultimately became his de facto diary. And later, as Rob and I began to interview his colleagues together—doctors, nurses, patient care technicians,* physician's assistants, and others—we found a commonality in the attempts by these healthcare workers to create order from chaos, manage an overwhelming workload, and cope with death, hopelessness, and survivor's guilt. I'm honored to have been able to work with my cousin to tell these remarkable stories that trace the onslaught of Covid-19 as it ripped through the Bronx in the spring of 2020, because ultimately they are stories of great heroism amidst deep despair.

For many medical professionals interviewed for this book, Rob and I were the first people they'd spoken to about their experiences. Over and over, we heard people express a desire to protect their husbands, wives, parents, and children from everything they had seen and done. To most, it was all too terrifying, in large part because they were forced by the circumstances to put themselves in danger. Alarmingly, especially early on, some had to reuse the

---

* The modern term for what used to be called an "orderly."

same masks and personal protective equipment for days on end. The risks they were taking, combined with the death surrounding them, were often too much for them to bear, and many of them, including Rob, frequently broke down and wept at the end of their shifts.

Rob explained to me how, on a chilly, wet night just before the official start of spring, he stepped outside onto the ambulance bay. The street, normally choked with vehicles, was almost empty. Traffic lights cycled green, yellow, and red, but without cars or buses to pass through them. The commuter railroad tracks that run adjacent to Montefiore's Weiler Campus were empty. But a group of people had congregated at the hospital's gates, and Rob could hear them voicing prayers in a half dozen languages for loved ones inside. These were family members who had been denied entry for fear of exposing them to the virus. Rob felt a mixture of grief and shame at having to walk by the group, at not being able to help, at not being able to offer the comfort that doctors are supposed to offer.

I won't lie, Rob texted me that night. *And I don't say it at home. Not to anyone. I break down and cry a lot. I don't like who I have become. Almost indifferent. Yet at the same time, I have been shown incredible compassion and sympathy. The elderly are my cross to bear, but I am holding the hands of young people, too—with the fear of God in their eyes like I have never seen.*

.   .   .

MONTEFIORE HOSPITAL'S WEILER CAMPUS, WHERE ROB works, sits at the center of all that is the Bronx. Geographically, this means the Bronx Zoo and the New York Botanical Garden are to the west; Pelham Bay Park and Long Island Sound are to the east. To the north, the Bronx becomes whiter and wealthier as the borough segues, not always evenly, into the even whiter environs of suburban Westchester County. South of the hospital, separated from Manhattan by the narrow expanse of the Harlem River, is the South Bronx. Known in the 1970s as a place where dozens of buildings burned, the area has been rebuilt, with more than nineteen thousand new apartments having been added since the 1980s.

Morris Park, the neighborhood Montefiore anchors, has a large Italian American population. The elements that keep it traditional also make it unique: the little coffeehouses; the shops where you can buy rice balls and fresh mozzarella. (In Morris Park, you never, ever pronounce the "a" at the end. It's "moo-*tsa*-rell.") But like the rest of the Bronx, Morris Park is home to a wide range of ethnicities, including large Hispanic and Black populations along with Albanians and Asian Americans. This is the part of the Bronx represented by Alexandria Ocasio-Cortez in Congress, its communities still reflecting the role the borough has played since the mid-nineteenth century: a place where people come to start life in America.

Like most modern hospitals, Montefiore isn't a single

place. It is instead a *system*, a sprawling patchwork of massive buildings, laboratories, private office towers, parking lots, classrooms, and even residences for some workers. Since it began serving the Bronx in 1912 (the first Montefiore was built in 1884 in Manhattan and was known as the Montefiore Home for Chronic Invalids), it has become the primary healthcare destination for 275,000 patients annually. It is also the borough's largest employer. The hospital stands adjacent to the affiliated Albert Einstein College of Medicine. Because of this, and given the huge number of patients it serves, it's a great place to learn, home to the nation's second-largest medical residency program. Doctors who work at Montefiore see everything, and they leave—whether to go to suburban hospitals, to other city facilities, or on missions overseas—ready for anything.

While the Bronx has made great strides in building and expanding its infrastructure—the culmination of that effort being the $2.3 billion renovation of Yankee Stadium, completed in 2009—the borough is still one of the poorest, least healthy urban counties in America. And most of the sickest people here are the working poor, who have limited access to medical services, nutritious food, quality education, childcare, and eldercare. The Bronx is also dotted with nursing homes, and maybe that's why, as Covid-19 descended on the borough in early 2020, Rob wondered whether he and the hospital were anywhere close to prepared.

Even in an emergency department like Montefiore's, where hundreds of thousands of patients receive treatment each year, there had never been anything like Covid-19. In the first of many messages Rob sent me, he likened the situation to a natural disaster. Patients were coming in by ambulance, in cars, on buses, even on foot, crowding the hospital's always-open entrances. New York's emergency medical response community, a weblike system that includes firefighters, paramedics, police, doctors, and hospitals, had been training for cataclysmic events since the terrorist attacks of September 11, 2001, and its Bronx-based armored command center is across the road from Montefiore's Weiler Campus. The members of this community were ready for a terrorist attack, a bombing, a mass shooting, even a chemical or biological attack, but they were not ready for a virus. Covid-19 is virulent. It is highly contagious. It can kill fast, sometimes within hours. No hospital in America was ready for that.

At Montefiore, every inch of empty space was requisitioned for Covid-19 patients, including all of the emergency rooms and, later, even many nonmedical areas. Rob described what I would later see for myself when I visited the hospitals: The sick and suffering on stretchers crowded together—crying, moaning, praying, and dying. People calling out in multiple languages for their mothers, children, God, lying often inches away from dead bodies that needed to be moved.

All of the staff—not just doctors and nurses but also attendants, security guards, respiratory therapists, and social workers—were in constant motion. Rob would move back and forth across the floor, checking in with colleagues who wore improvised scrubs, paper gowns, painting and welding masks, even hazmat coveralls. One doctor provided unintentional comic relief by showing up in what looked like a beekeeper's suit. Human voices struggled to rise above the thrum of artificial breathing apparatuses, the cacophony of electronic beeps punctuating the low pumping sound of mimicked exhalations.

Everywhere, hard discussions had to take place: Telling a parent that their child was dying but visiting was impossible because of the risk of infection. Telling a child that their parent, who had barely exhibited symptoms a day earlier, wasn't going to make it. These conversations impacted the doctors and nurses along with the patients, the well along with the sick. The sadness was inescapable.

During those first weeks, Rob's sorrow was inescapable, too. Sometimes, when he'd send me a text or a voicemail, I'd feel as if he was channeling not just what he felt but also the pain of all those who were suffering, all those who'd lost someone.

Rob and I are related not just by blood but by a deep bond between our fathers. Born eight months apart, they were first cousins who grew up more like brothers, often describing themselves as "near-identical twins." Later, they would bring Rob and me together as kids. But it wasn't until 2012, when my father was dying, that my deepest connection with Rob was forged.

My father had been an emergency room doctor himself and had given Rob his first job, mentoring him in diagnostics, ethics, and clinical practice. When my dad became ill—the official diagnosis was "cancer of unknown primary," or CUP, meaning the disease had spread everywhere in his body from seemingly nowhere—he left his medical decisions to Rob and expressed very clearly that he never wanted to be put on a ventilator. When he was unable to breathe on his own following a lung biopsy, he had to be put on one anyway. When the doctors attempted to remove the device, a process called weaning, it was a messy failure, leaving his bed in the ICU spattered with blood. I stood in the corner, in shock, until the doctors noticed I was there and gently escorted me out.

My brother and I didn't know what to do. So we called Rob, who was traveling with his family on the other side of the world. He laid out the medical facts and then explained that since he was overseas and unable to examine Richard in person, we had to make the decision ourselves. As secondary medical proxy, my brother signed off on the agonizing choice to let my father die. I can tell you, then, from firsthand knowledge, that dying on a ventilator is a horrific experience. Seeing it once in my lifetime was enough for me. In the first twelve weeks of the Covid pandemic, Rob and his colleagues would see it multiple times each day.

· · ·

THIS BOOK CHRONICLES THE ONSET, IN ONE COMMUNITY, OF A disease so novel and so brutal that every physician learned to cope with it not with the measured, data-based techniques of modern medicine, but by trial and error, email, blog posts, and networking with other doctors. At one point, Rob told me, his voice cracking with sadness, "People are dying because nobody knows what to do." The truth is more subtle. Covid-19 imposed a steep and tragic learning curve. The only thing doctors could do was do their best.

This is not just the story of a disease. It is not simply a medical drama. This is a record of grief. Many people have died, and many of the people who have died of Covid-19, all over the world, have died alone. With that sorrow and anguish in mind, this is the story of an emergency room team that struggled to care for their patients, did everything they could, and still, too often, witnessed their patients' deaths.

Between when we started this book, in March 2020, and when the first draft of this manuscript was finished, six months later, more than six thousand people were treated for Covid-19 at Montefiore. Almost one thousand died.

Goodbyes were hard to come by in March and April. So were proper burials. The dead were reduced to ashes at New York's public crematoria or buried in mass graves on Hart Island, a small dot of land in Long Island Sound between Manhattan, Queens, and the Bronx. In that anonymous but hallowed ground, they joined the victims of influenza, smallpox, cholera, and typhus. (The infamous Mary Mallon, known as "Typhoid Mary," was quarantined for decades on one of the islands in that narrow, brackish channel.)

This book is written in Rob's voice, but it is not only his story. It's the story of the struggle to tip the balance in favor of life over death. It's the narrative of heroic medical professionals who risked their own lives to save as many of their patients as they could. Above all, the goal of this book, as has been stated repeatedly by those same brave doctors, nurses, and support staff, is to honor those who couldn't be saved during that first terrible, tragic Covid spring.

Dan Koeppel
Portland, Maine, September 2020

PART I

March 2020

When a novel virus was first identified in Wuhan, China, in December 2019*—with the first reported death following on January 11, 2020—there was little concern at hospitals and healthcare facilities in the United States. Nor was there alarm on January 19, when a thirty-five-year-old man, just back from a visit to Wuhan, reported to a Washington State health clinic with symptoms similar to those seen in China: a cough and vomiting. The patient was held for eight days before being released from the hospital, and while he was being treated, a U.S. Centers for Disease Control press release focused on the patient's recent travels and was equivocal

---

* The exact date is the source of some dispute, but by mid-December, it's almost certain infections were spreading in Wuhan.

about whether the disease could be easily transmitted: "While originally thought to be spreading from animal-to-person, there are growing indications that limited person-to-person spread is happening. It's unclear how easily this virus is spreading between people."

At the end of January, the World Health Organization declared a global emergency as the total number of global cases reached nine thousand. During this time, doctors at Montefiore began hearing stories: An urgent care doctor in Queens had a patient who had returned from a vacation in China with flu-like symptoms. One doctor reported that he'd sent information about a patient to the CDC but had gotten no response. It had been a mild flu season. For the most part, patients presenting in urban emergency rooms with flu-like symptoms were being treated for influenza and were surviving.

Even on March 1, when New York governor Andrew Cuomo announces that a thirty-nine-year-old woman who recently traveled to Iran has the virus and has been forced into isolation at home, few doctors are thinking about Covid-19. By early March, however, the CDC has confirmed that at least sixty people in the United States have been infected with the virus. The cases appear to be isolated. Almost half are travelers, many passengers on a cruise ship forced to dock off Japan when the disease broke out. Those unfortunate vacationers are sequestered offshore for two weeks, then flown back to the United States, where they are again quarantined at an Air Force base in Texas.

The idea that one can catch Covid from somebody who hasn't been overseas or hasn't been around clusters of the disease is still not broadly accepted.

The reckoning begins in the New York suburb of New Rochelle, where the first concentration of cases and the first confirmed instance of community transmission in the United States occurs. "Patient zero" is a fifty-year-old man, and ten other cases soon follow. This leads Governor Cuomo to declare a mandatory lockdown. Nearby schools shutter—in hopes that the closures will be brief, allowing just enough time for them to be sanitized—and Cuomo says that while the disease will spread, panic is unnecessary: "If you understand the facts, there is no reason for undue anxiety. There are going to be dozens and dozens and dozens of people. And the more people you test, the more people you're going to find." On March 5, 11 new cases are reported in New York City, while the United States has 172 cases total, 12 of which have resulted in death.

At Montefiore, it starts slowly, with just three patients admitted across the hospital system by the end of the first week of March. But then the numbers begin to grow exponentially: Two dozen by mid-March. Approximately two hundred a week later. More than a thousand a week after that.

Montefiore's Covid patients are among the sickest in the city, due in part to the community Montefiore serves. A quick search for "nursing homes" within a two-mile radius of any of Montefiore's main campuses yields more than fifty facilities. Statistics supplied by New York State indicate that there are at least five thousand elderly people in those facilities, nearly all vulnerable because of their age and preexisting conditions. Those nursing homes begin to send their sickest clients to Montefiore's emergency rooms. One study shows that more than 60 percent of those testing positive at the hospital for Covid are Black or Hispanic.

Despite all this, Montefiore's doctors remain confident early on that they can handle whatever happens. They believe in their training, in their equipment, and in their mission, which is to care for the people of the Bronx. But very quickly, the flood of patients—now not just elderly folks from nursing homes, but the sons and daughters and friends and neighbors of those initial victims—threatens to overrun even this sprawling, modern medical facility.

Chapter One

I t's the second Saturday in March, and Governor Andrew Cuomo has just declared a state of emergency, but if you were to look out the doors of the hospital, you'd agree that the word "emergency" is an understatement. Ambulance after ambulance is lined up on Eastchester Road, blocking the drive-throughs at Starbucks and McDonald's, continuing on toward the elevated railroad tracks and beyond. I can't even see the end of the line. Staff arriving for work can't get close enough to the hospital to park there because of the ambulances snaking around the block, idling as they wait.

The nursing homes that surround us can do a lot to treat their own patients, and normally we encounter one of their residents only after a major incident like a heart attack or a fall. But now it feels like we're seeing all of them. Patients are coming in on stretchers and in wheelchairs with "air hunger"—so starved for oxygen that they're gasping. Often their families have been notified, so the sick person will wait with anxious sons and daughters, brothers and sisters. Confused relatives wander down the row of ambulances trying to find their loved ones. Today, the entrance to the ER is so crowded that we have to get security to clear it.

"They're just unloading on us," one of my colleagues says.

It gets worse after the patients are checked in. Many people who can't get enough air need to be put on ventilators that will breathe for them, and we're concerned that we don't have enough vents. So we've had to form an ethics committee—unprecedented in my experience—to determine what we'll do if the ventilator supply runs dry.

Ventilators require intubation, an art emergency medicine doctors spend a lot of time perfecting. An endotracheal tube must be inserted down a patient's throat and through the vocal cords. Over the years, the practice has evolved from direct laryngeal intubation—where you basically insert the tube into the airway by sight—to fiber-optic guided intubation, which is a lot more successful. As emergency room doctors, we pride ourselves on being the best at intubating in a crisis, but a lot of factors affect how well an intubation will go. It's harder with obese patients, ones with shorter necks, and those with trauma.

Often a patient in an emergency room is surrounded by a half dozen people—doctors, nurses, physician's assistants, respiratory therapists—when they're being intubated. There's stuff coming up from their lungs, and the doctor's face is right over the patient's open mouth, getting sprayed with respiratory secretions. Sometimes the patient vomits. The moment of intubation is probably the most exposed a doctor can ever be.

Although emergency room doctors can intubate in a crunch, your average anesthesiologist can do it five times more efficiently, because that's what they do all day. If you've ever been put under general anesthesia, you've been intubated. Anesthesiologists normally come down to the ER only when we call them in on difficult cases. With the virus spreading quickly, we want them down here performing all our intubations. But the people upstairs don't understand what's happening in the emergency room. Even though they're just a few floors above us, they aren't seeing what we are seeing. Up there, the status quo still applies.

WE'RE RUNNING OUT OF SPACE. I DO A QUICK COUNT, AND there are more than seventy Covid patients in the ER. That's more than double the number we have room for in the zone we dedicated to Covid care just a few days earlier. And they're still coming. These patients, who we know have an infectious disease, are all crowded up against one another. They're crying. They're praying. And they're dying.

Nearly all emergency rooms have something called a

diversion plan—a predetermined strategy to get the sickest people to another location where they can be seen sooner. Maybe the diversion lasts for an hour, maybe for two hours, maybe, if things are really bad, for a whole day. But in my twenty-five years as an emergency room doctor in the Bronx, I've never called for diversion. Montefiore, as a matter of policy, never closes its doors to the community. It's not what we do. We don't turn people away. Ever.

At the same time, we've never had a Chernobyl before. And that's what this feels like: a nuclear disaster. I look over at the big yellow milk-crate-sized cases that hold our dwindling supply of ventilators. I don't want to think about what will happen if we run out.

EMERGENCY ROOM PERSONNEL HAVE A JOB THAT SEEMS, ON the surface, rather narrow: We're fundamentally about the first sixty minutes of the medical encounter, a period we call the golden hour. We triage, treat, and stabilize, and then move the patient on to the next step—sometimes to another part of the hospital, sometimes home. We rehearse for that golden hour in so many ways. But we don't train for the type of systemic failure we're now experiencing.

We have more patients than our team can handle. But we can't call for diversion, and it's not just a matter of policy. The other hospitals nearby are going through the same thing. We are all being crushed. There's no place to divert to.

This failure hurts. Because the thing is, I love this hospital, and I love the Bronx. Sometimes working here is like working in a foreign country, and it's not just the twenty-five languages that are spoken here. (We translate all of them, through staff who speak different languages or via telephone linkups.) At Montefiore, we see everything ten-fold: every hurt, every disease. Some emergency room doctors in the Bronx see more gunshot and stab wounds in a year than most doctors outside New York City and other big urban centers see in their entire careers—although our emergency room doesn't get a lot of those, since there's a Level I Trauma Center at Jacobi Medical Center right across the street that's better equipped to handle patients with such injuries.

After I had been working here for a while, I noticed that patients started putting my colleagues and me down on forms as their primary care doctors. We're not, but they know us. They know we'll treat their hyperglycemia when they can't afford their insulin. We'll treat their asthma. They know that we'll never refuse them a bed when it's cold or they're hungry. It makes me feel proud that they see us as the place they can turn to. But right now, that pride is being crushed by fear.

EARLY IN MY SHIFT, A YOUNG PATIENT NAMED ARTHUR, ABOUT thirty years old, waves me over. It's hectic in the ER, but I feel the need to connect with patients no matter how busy it is. So I walk over and sit on the edge of his bed.

The first thing he does is show me a picture of his kids, and it's a good move on his part, because I am instantly drawn in. I also have kids, though his are younger. He tells me the oldest one is seven years old, and he's been dealing with kidney failure. His son is on peritoneal dialysis, which means he has catheters coming out of his belly to remove fluid. Either he or his wife has to manage this, or the boy will die.

I take a quick look at Arthur's chart and see that he's reporting that he hasn't felt well for two weeks. That's a long time. He's an electrician, and he's been out of work. He's been quarantining in the bathroom of the tiny apartment where he lives with his wife and sick child, afraid to come to the ER.

"I've basically been managing my care through 311," he says. He's been calling the New York City public information line to figure out what he needs to do if he has certain symptoms—when he can go to work, when he has to stay home. He learned that he could go back to work only if he had a doctor's note saying he was okay. Then he tells me something that really stuns me.

"I started out with $3,100 in my bank account, Doc," he says. "I was down to $4, so I had to do it."

"Had to do what?"

"I figured out what the doctor's note needed to say, and I wrote it myself."

He looks at me, and tears start rolling down his face.

The letter didn't work. They saw how sick he was and sent him home.

He has lucked out in that he has pneumonia, not Covid, but he doesn't know if he is going to be allowed back to work, given his health status. He has an empty bank account and a sick child. What is he going to do?

COVID DOESN'T PUT ONLY *PATIENTS'* LIVES AT RISK. IT'S A danger to all of us who work at the hospital. I find myself feeling contempt for them, which is something I have never experienced during my entire career, and I'm ashamed of it. How can a doctor be resentful toward a bunch of sick people? It's not their fault.

The patients from the nursing homes didn't ask to be brought here. We're giving them Tylenol, fluids, and hydroxychloroquine, which seems like a promising remedy but will later be discredited. We're giving them lots of oxygen, through a face mask or nasal cannula. We intubate them. And still so many die.

We don't have solid guidelines, and we're struggling with the very thing we're trained to do: save people's lives. In a world of evidence-based medicine, an unprecedented event like this puts us at a disadvantage. And maybe— though we're too busy to truly worry about it right now—we know we could have done a better job anticipating this, preventing this.

We'd gotten something of a warning in the form of vague reports from friends working at other hospitals in other cities. In early March, one of my medical school buddies who practices in Los Angeles had an alarming case: A guy in his midforties came in with breathing problems. He was tested three times for Covid, the tests came back negative all three times, and he wasn't confirmed as having had Covid until after he was dead. There was nothing they could do to save him. Another one of my colleagues who moonlights at a walk-in clinic in Queens is convinced that he was seeing cases in December. But there was no test back then. So despite these murmurings, we were blindsided. Like so many people in this country, we believed that the virus was far away and would stay far away. It was in China, in other foreign countries, but it wasn't going to come to the United States.

Even the New Rochelle cases seemed distant, somehow, though I live just minutes from that town. An acquaintance told me about a man from his congregation who'd gotten ill. That man turned out to be the state's infamous "patient zero." But maybe because the news came from a friend rather than a public report, I didn't think about the situation from an epidemiological perspective. To me it seemed like an isolated event at the time. In fact, I had been so dismissive that when I received a text from my buddy Charles in February asking, *Doc, is this coronavirus thing going to be a big deal?* my clueless response was, *Nah, no different than the flu.*

I've never been more wrong in my life.

At the start, all I knew was that a woman in New York who'd traveled overseas had gotten sick, and then two more people were sick, and then nine people. But I didn't worry. I mean, the mayor of New York was riding the subway to show how *not* concerned he was. Even when the number of cases in New York hit one hundred—when I knew that we'd be seeing Covid in our hospital—I still didn't understand.

Then came the night of March 6, just before my first weekend shift of the month, when I received a text from a young registration clerk at our hospital named Amanda. She's great, always helpful and fun, and once taught me how to set up my cable box so I could watch more sports. Her text said: *The Blue Zone is now the Covid Zone.* Our facility has always sectioned its emergency room into four zones: Blue, White, Red, and Green. Most large emergency rooms are divided into similar zones, and at Montefiore, Red is for the most critical patients, while White and Blue are for patients who have less urgent problems but need care fairly soon. The difference is that Blue is for patients who can't move under their own power, and White is for patients who can. The Green Zone is for urgent care, rather than emergent: cuts, scrapes, sore throats, earaches. We can treat these problems and then send the patients home. But a single diagnosis had never encompassed an entire zone of the hospital before.

That night, I lay awake picturing what my next day

would look like: maybe like a really bad shift during a typical flu season, the zone full of older people, doctors checking their comorbidities, doing what needed to be done, moving on to the next patient. But I was still in denial. The next morning, I walked into the emergency room the same as always: no mask, no gloves. I was invincible. And I still didn't want to think that Covid could happen here.

Now, as my twelve-hour shift is coming to an end, I look at the triage number—the patients needing to be screened—and it keeps going up. Kyle, an attending physician not long out of residency, comes in to take over the care of the patients I've been tending to during my shift. Normally, this would mean a detailed discussion about what every patient might need over the next few hours, but Covid has thrown that protocol out the window. It's down to a single question, and Kyle asks, "Who do I intubate first?"

"The one whose oxygen saturation is lowest," I say.

Kyle is one of the hardest-working doctors I've ever met. He'll often log on to our case management system at home, just to know what he's going to face when his shift starts. I instantly wonder whether I spoke to him too abruptly. I'm going to have to figure out a way to manage the stress, because I'm coming to understand that this is just the beginning.

.   .   .

WHEN I'M BACK FOR MY NEXT SHIFT, THINGS HAVE GOTTEN worse. My first patient is an eighty-one-year-old man named Lopez who is running a fever of 105. That's pretty much as bad as it gets. We hook him up to a pulse oximeter, and as the little clamp closes around his finger, his blood oxygen reading makes alarms go off. Normal saturation levels are 96 percent or higher. If you draw a 90 percent reading, that's really bad. Lopez is at 78 percent. Plus, he's burning up, and his chest X-ray shows that his lungs are filled with fluid, indicating bilateral pneumonia. It's the same reading we're getting on patient after patient. These numbers basically mean that he has barely any chance of survival, and yet, somehow, he's awake. He's alert. He's talking to me. He tells me that his granddaughter is a doctor, but she couldn't come because she's fighting cancer herself. I'm staggered.

Lopez has a DNI/DNR order, which means "do not intubate/do not resuscitate." The data on survival rates for older people being put on ventilators is incomplete, but various studies would ultimately show that as few as 10 percent to as many as 50 percent of Covid patients who ended up on a ventilator didn't make it. That matches up with our rapidly evolving clinical experience. Those kinds of odds have to be terrifying, even if you've got a strong will to live.

I ask Lopez if the DNI/DNR order in his records is a true reflection of his wishes. He tells me that it is, that he understands what it means. Even so, I place the usual Covid orders—for oxygen and Tylenol—and then take a deep breath as I move on to the next patient. And the next and the next. An hour later, one of the nurses tracks me down.

"Lopez is dead," she says. He came in at 1:45 P.M. He was pronounced dead at 4:30. He was sent to the morgue at 6:00. He didn't suffer, I hope.

I NEED TO TAKE A BREAK. IT FEELS LIKE EVERY MONITOR IN the hospital is beeping, everybody's talking at once, and patients are moaning and coughing all around me. I step outside, and suddenly I feel like my knees are going to buckle. Then I'm crying.

I think to call my buddy Pete. He was head of security at the hospital for decades and was in charge of ambulances, but now he's retired. He's a big guy, six feet eight, with just the attitude you'd expect from a guy with that job: no bullshit. We met when I got caught stealing M&M's from the hospital kitchen by the head of nutrition. Pete called me into his office and said, "What are we going to do about this?" I felt like a kid in grade school—until he laughed. He'd seen the incriminating video that showed me stealing the candy but also showed me giving it to patients and their families. Since then, Pete has been my voice of reason. I've called him for advice on everything from how to deal with patients to how to deal with my own children, and he's never steered me wrong. Pete picks up on the first ring.

"How you doin', Doc?" I can tell by the way he asks that he knows, and I lose control and start sobbing.

"How do I make this go away?" I ask him.

"You're not gonna do that," he says. "Put your poker face on. Pull yourself together."

He pauses for a second. "Don't go back until you're ready," he says, "but you're going back."

I take another minute, and then I walk back in. As I do, I look at the ambulances, the EMTs, the swarms of people, and that's when it hits me: This is worse than anything I've ever imagined.

When I teach residents about handling death, I start with advance directives. What does that term mean? We've all thought about what happens at the end of life, and we probably all have a sense of how we'd want medical decisions to be made if we couldn't make them ourselves. As a doctor, your job is not to judge. Your job is to act in service of the patient's wishes. This takes on a new meaning when you see a patient who is fighting against all odds, who you know is going to die anyway.

And there are more challenges to interacting with patients now: How can you act in their best interests when you're wearing a face mask and a face shield and are draped in Tyvek? You can't easily talk to them. You can't explain the decisions of life and death. And when you face an emergency room where it seems like everybody is dying, where there's no room to move, where every patient is gasping for air, you just can't be the doctor you want to be.

I feel this all acutely when the hardest case of the day comes at the end of it: a fifty-three-year-old woman who is morbidly obese and asthmatic and is running a fever. She arrived with an oxygen saturation level of 100 percent, but two hours later it has dropped to 60 percent. We put her on supplemental oxygen through a mask. I stand over her, monitoring the readout and experiencing another kind of anxiety, knowing her family will be calling soon. And sure enough, her daughter calls in to the ER. I'm obliged to put her on speakerphone, since we've been told not to touch the telephones. Our conversation is nearly drowned out by all the background noise and not nearly as private as it should be.

"How's my mom?" the daughter asks.

"We're doing everything we can," I say. My medical judgment is that her mom isn't going to survive. I know how much hearing that would hurt. I've been on the other side of the conversation.

In my first year of medical school, I received a phone call telling me that my mom and dad had been in a car accident. A drunk driver swerved into their lane, causing a head-on collision. When I got to the hospital, I was told my dad was in and out of consciousness. I saw them working on my mom while she was still on the gurney from the ambulance that had brought her in. An hour later, she was pronounced dead.

That's something you never really get over. The last gift my mom gave me was a pair of green Chuck Taylors. I wore them for years—throughout medical school, my internship, my residency. I wore them until they fell apart. Maybe so *I* wouldn't.

But I finally had to toss those sneakers, and a friend at the hospital who knew how much they meant to me bought me another pair. Then someone else gave me a pair, and it got to be a regular thing. Now I don't just have green ones. I have Chuck Taylors with American flags. With Bart Simpson. With glitter. Even patients have given them to me. My current pair has my name monogrammed on one side of each shoe, with a line from *Porgy and Bess,* "Summertime and the living is easy," on the other. I've never gone in to work in anything other than those sneakers. So my mom is always with me. She was proud that I chose to become a doctor, and I know she'd tell me to do my job, even if it hurts.

I look down at my feet as I respond to the daughter's questions, knowing what it feels like to face the fact that your mother will most likely die, when all you want is for her to live. I wish I could assure this woman that her mother will be fine. It hurts not to be able to say something that will ease her pain. More than just about any other time in my career, I feel completely helpless.

.   .   .

THE LAST THING I DO BEFORE I LEAVE WORK IS RETURN TO this patient who I've been hoping won't need a ventilator. I've shown her how to read the pulse oximeter and said: "Listen. Cough. Take deep breaths. You keep that number over 90 percent, and you keep yourself off the ventilator." But when I leave, she is very close to dropping below that. I feel bad because I know she'll likely need to be intubated, and I've left that job for the next doctor.

But I'm anxious to get home to my wife, Janet, and to our little house at the far end of a cul-de-sac. I already have a ritual to keep from infecting my family: I change my clothes in the hospital parking lot. When I get home, I strip naked in the garage and streak straight to the shower, where I scrub myself from head to toe. I even wash my mouth and nose out with hot, soapy water.

This evening, I fly up the Saw Mill River Parkway at 70 miles per hour. The sun is setting to my left, along a section of the road where the traffic hits the glare and there are often accidents. I always slow down to see if I'm needed, but not today. No car wrecks. No cars. The whole ride takes about twenty minutes, and by the time I'm home and cleaned up, my kids have arrived, both sent home from their campuses in favor of remote classes. My daughter, Bobbi, is about to finish college, and she's going to start medical school in the fall. She's always wanted to be a doctor. When she was a kid, I'd bring home my suture kits so she could practice on hot dogs and pigs' feet. Matt's aiming for a degree in health sciences. He just got home from Boston. It'll be the first time in years that we've all lived in the same house together. I'm glad they're going to be home, but I worry—and nearly everyone who works at the hospital who has loved ones at home feels the same way—that I'm going to get them sick.

Despite those fears, my kids remain my glimmer of hope, and that's something I need. They are the light glowing at the end of what may turn out to be the longest tunnel of my life. I've always believed I can do anything, endure anything, as long as I know there's an end point, as long as I know the rules. But today, there is no end point, and the rules? They're out the window.

Chapter Two

When I arrive four days later at seven in the morning for my next shift—it's the second Saturday in March—I'm told that we're running out of places to put the bodies. The morgue is full. And the funeral homes have been nearly shut down out of fear of spreading the disease among mourners. The white, standard-issue body bags that preserve a corpse for only a few days have been replaced by heavy-duty, bright orange ones while we wait for refrigerated trucks to arrive.

Some of the bodies are so heavy the attendants can't lift them on their own. I overhear one ask how he's supposed to manage all this. It wouldn't be right to drag the bags. We can't treat human beings that way. But using two people is a drain on resources. Nonetheless, we recruit hospital attendants and other personnel who, as is obvious from the horror in their eyes, have little experience with the dead. Some of the bereaved watch as we load the trucks. This hauling away of orange bags becomes the last point of contact for a good number of people whose sons and daughters, husbands and wives, weren't allowed to visit them, weren't given the chance to say goodbye.

The Covid Zone (formerly the Blue Zone) has beds for as many as twenty-five patients, and even on normal days before the virus, we often had stretchers doubled up. Our standard capacity allows for as many as forty patients during busy times. Right now, we have almost twice that many. Cardiac monitors are blaring, and in the atmosphere-controlled negative pressure rooms, people are being venti-lated. (These rooms are like an inflated inner tube, where no air can get in or out except through a single valve. This prevents almost anything *in* the air, like microscopic virus particles, from ingress or egress as well.) Some patients are praying; others are vomiting; still others are propped in wheelchairs, forced to use bedpans in these very crowded conditions because, we are learning, Covid-19 causes diar-rhea. It's our job to maneuver around the X-ray machines and get to them all. Normally, before an X-ray is taken, everybody gets out of the way after the tech calls for the all clear. This morning there is none of that. Every patient needs to have their lungs checked. Nowhere is clear, so it's radiation for all.

A husband and wife are brought in together. I'm guess-ing they're both in their eighties and, from their accents, that they probably came to the Bronx from somewhere in Latin America. They're both robust, solid people, far from what you'd call infirm. They're dressed up, like the virus has caught them by surprise in the middle of a celebration. But they're really sick, and they arrive by ambulance because they need help breathing. We can't treat them together. The husband is in worse shape, so he'll get intubated first. We explain this to them, though they're probably both in shock. They don't know how ill they are, and later I will wonder if this is the first evidence we've seen of the neurological effects that we'll soon discover so many Covid patients frequently suffer. As they're wheeling the husband away, the wife is looking over her shoulder, and I can tell that she's trying to wave, but she's too weak to move.

I have a feeling in the pit of my stomach of not having done enough to prepare them for what is to come. This could be the last time they see each other. They've likely been together for fifty years or more. At his age, the husband probably needs glasses, and he isn't wearing them. He probably couldn't even see the sad expression on his wife's face. Her condition is deteriorating by the minute, which is the nature of the virus: Patients go from seemingly fine to not fine very quickly. There's no option but to put her on a ventilator, even though the odds are that she won't ever get off it. The saddest thing is that they parted as if one of them was going to work or the grocery store, like they were going to see each other again.

We have four ventilators that aren't in use when a man

in his fifties, more lucid than many others I have seen, comes in. He has asthma. He's overweight. He says he stayed at home until he felt like he couldn't breathe. He's wearing a shirt that says "Quinnipiac Baseball." I'm a baseball fanatic. I grew up in Queens, home of the Mets. I work in the Bronx, home of the Yankees. But I'm a lifelong Red Sox fan because my mom was. So, of course, I ask. It turns out his son will graduate from high school this spring and start college in the fall at Quinnipiac University in Connecticut, where he'll play baseball as an outfielder. Almost the same age as my son, Matthew. The patient shows me a video of his kid hitting and throwing at a pro tryout. He looks me in the eye and says, "Doc, I just want to see my son play baseball again. Save me a vent."

I can't say no, so I promise him, no matter what I have to do, that there's going to be a vent for him. Guaranteed. But "Baseball Dad" isn't even in line to receive one. As I'm making this promise, another patient gets wheeled in.

Mr. Franklin is in his mideighties, and he's in bad shape. He needs air, right now, and that means a vent, but he has a do not intubate/do not resuscitate order. As I'm reading through his chart, security calls up to say that his son has been waiting outside and would like to see his father. Meanwhile, I'm hearing from the staff that New York State Police vehicles are lined up outside the hospital. I'm wondering what that's about when a trooper, apparently high-ranking from the details on his uniform, comes up to me and says, "Let's do this."

I'm about to tell the trooper that it's probably too risky for him to enter the hospital, but he raises his hand. "Don't bother," he says. "I'm going in."

That's when I make the connection. This is Franklin's son, the guy security called me about a few minutes ago. "Why didn't you let somebody know?" I ask him. "It would have gotten you in sooner."

"Not my style," he says.

"You should know that your father is in critical condition," I tell him, but his expression doesn't change.

I don't know if I've ever seen a cop cry. Or a son cry the way this man does as he stands over his father. It's heartbreaking.

When I leave them to check on my other patients, my thoughts return to the promise I made to Baseball Dad, and I wonder, *Will Franklin want a ventilator for his father?* Even with the signed DNI/DNR, he'd be within his rights to demand that he get one.

But that's not what Franklin Jr. does. He doesn't ask me about his father's chances of survival. He doesn't try to intervene in his father's passing.

We still have ventilators available. That means every patient who needs one, gets one. At least for now, we're not being forced to ration. But we're scared that we're heading toward the time when we'll have to pick and choose who gets one and who doesn't, and that's a doctor's worst nightmare.

Down the hall, I recognize the soft sound of sobbing: Another relative has slipped through security.

"My name is Dr. Meyer," I say to her, suppressing the instinct to extend my gloved hand. She acknowledges my presence by trying to fight back the tears. I can't really see her face because she's wearing a mask, but I'm starting to think that I'm the problem, that I've done something wrong.

"Meyer is my dad's first name," she says. And she tells me the story of her father, how he was fine until he broke his hip. Then something went wrong in the surgery, he ended up in a nursing home, and now he's dead. I give her a minute before I ask if there's anything I can do.

"Is there any way you can take this stuff out of him?" she asks. He's still connected to an IV and an endotracheal tube, so I disconnect everything. Then she says, "But his mouth. It's wide open. Why?"

My first thought is to explain rigor mortis to her. Then I think of my friend Angelo Recine. Angelo is a plumber and one of the most carefree people I know. Some people know him by his profession, and sure, he'll come over to my house to unclog a drain. But he'll start by opening a bottle of wine, and then he'll have a glass along with some cheese before he gets to the job at hand. He's got his priorities straight.

I took care of his mother in the ER for more than a decade before she passed away a year ago. When I showed up at her beside for the last time, Angelo was just sitting there. He wasn't crying; he was just very still. She was old, so her dying wasn't a complete shock. But something else was bothering him. I could tell. It turns out Angelo couldn't stand to see the way her mouth had dropped open, which is what happens when rigor mortis sets in.

He asked me if I had any gauze. I found some and handed it to him. He proceeded to tie it around her head to keep her jaw in place. He said he'd learned this as a kid growing up in Italy: white fabric or linen wrapped under the chin to give the deceased a modicum of dignity. So I use Angelo's old-world trick on Meyer. I tie some material around his head, looping it under his chin, making sure to leave his face exposed.

I wish I could stay for a while, spend time with his daughter, learn more about him, but I get a page from Medical Records and have to excuse myself. They need me to complete some paperwork so that the bodies can be taken away. I wish I could hand this task off to a resident, but it's hospital protocol. Residents don't sign death certificates. Attendings do. And for some reason, I'm the go-to guy here.

Typically when I go to a deceased patient's room, I ask the team who has treated the patient if they have any objections to pronouncing the death. They've already tried resuscitation through CPR, which includes chest compressions. If they say no, I document the time of death and sign the certificate—all recorded electronically these days. Every doc has their own way of doing this. Death is traumatic. We all need closure. But now we're so busy that the process is compressed, though no less difficult.

On the way upstairs, I pass Kyle performing CPR. I'm gone fifteen, maybe twenty, minutes, and when I return, he's still resuscitating the patient. So I pause. I know what he's feeling. Somebody he was just treating has coded, and he's trying to keep that person alive. But he's lost this battle.

"It's time to stop," I tell him, trying not to sound as if I'm issuing a command.

Kyle stops and looks up at me incredulously. I can see, even beneath the layers of gear—or maybe because of them—that he's sweating. I feel sick. Who am I to tell him to give up? He looks away.

Emergency room doctors see a lot of death. It comes with the territory. Even so, we try to make our job, our career, about life.

I'M SURPRISED WHEN I WALK OUTSIDE AND SEE THAT TRIAGE is now taking place in a tent that's arrived and been put up during my shift. I can hear the hum of the nearby condensers that keep the emergency room supplied with oxygen. It's a chilly March day, and the nurses are bundled up, wearing sweaters under their protective gear, as they examine the steady stream of arriving patients. We've become a welcome center for the walk-ins—the people who show up because they feel sick but are not transported by ambulance.

Everybody entering the hospital needs to be screened for Covid. The protocol is necessary so that incoming patients who don't have the virus don't get infected.

It's a massive operation. If a patient arrives in obvious respiratory distress, they're brought right into the emergency room and given oxygen. Everyone else has to pass through the tent. The hospital staff is gowned up, rubber gloves and masks on, not an inch of flesh showing—it's almost become a game to figure out who you're talking to. The only exceptions to the full PPE protocol are the city EMTs, who remain in their standard uniforms: no gowns and definitely no masks.

"They get in the way," one of them tells me when I remind him that he needs to take precautions. "We've got dozens of calls to answer." He shrugs.

The EMTs are throwing themselves into the abyss without regard for their own health. Some docs get angry that they're not taking the proper precautions, but I don't think they deserve the criticism. Sure, they need to be safe, but we should be pinning medals on their chests, not chastising them.

The tent is progress. Doing triage outside the ER frees up much-needed space inside. Far fewer living patients mixed in with the dead. This morning I heard a woman screaming, "Get this body away from me!" I knew she wasn't crazy, seeing dead people where there were none, just sick and stuck in place.

Most of the people outside won't be allowed inside the

ER. They'll wait in the tent for their vitals to be taken, and if their blood oxygen level is over 92 percent, they'll be sent home. "Come back if your symptoms get worse" is today's most often repeated phrase, and it's hard to believe we're saying it. We want people to come to the emergency room when they're sick. Nobody having a heart attack or a stroke should risk staying home because they might get Covid. But there's a real chance that if they show up at the ER, they'll get the virus, and for some people—especially many of the patients our hospital serves—that could be a death sentence. The idea now is to fill the emergency room only with people who really need to be there, which means those who really need care right now, whether they've got Covid or some other ailment.

"Really sick" is a term one often hears in the Bronx because many patients come to us with their health already compromised. There are sixty-two counties in New York State, and the Bronx—the state's poorest—is ranked first in health factors that contribute to decreased life spans. This is a result of a host of factors, including poor diet and lack of availability of nutritious food, which lead to obesity and diabetes; delayed care because people don't have primary care physicians, making their chronic conditions more debilitating; and smoking-related conditions such as asthma, emphysema, and COPD (chronic obstructive pulmonary disease). We want more people to be healthy, but an emergency room—which is designed to treat patients when things are at peak urgency—can't solve the bigger problems. And now many of those who are already sick are showing up with Covid. It's a deadly mix.

Two swabbing stations have been set up inside the tent for testing, and I take a minute to watch the incoming patients being tested. There are two different swabbing techniques: one nostril or, as recommended by the CDC, both nostrils and the oropharynx, which is the back of the throat. The swab should be really flexible, and the goal is to work your way along the floor of the nose until the swab gets to the mouth. If you open somebody's mouth while they're being swabbed, you might see the end of the swab way in back.

Some people say that it feels like the swab is going into their brain—it hurts that much—but it actually goes straight back to the nasal floor. A lot of practitioners are hesitant to put it in that far, and I get it. It's invasive and exceedingly uncomfortable. And for every patient who takes it like a champ, there are five swatting your hand away and writhing in pain, making it difficult to get a good test. Swabbing can also be dangerous for the practitioner. How can anybody not cough and gag when a giant swab is shoved up their nose? If a patient starts coughing, boom, the swabber is exposed. The instinct toward self-preservation is natural. But when the tests are done wrong, they lead to a lot of false negatives.

The test results change nothing in the short term, and not just because—at this stage of the pandemic—they can take several hours. If someone has an oxygen saturation level below 96 percent *and* symptoms that look like Covid, we treat them as though they have Covid and move them into the hospital.

On my way out of the tent, I'm stopped by two EMTs who are in an intense discussion with an older woman. I quickly figure out what's going on. She's seventy-four, upset, and crying. The EMTs say that she found her daughter dead in her room at home. They say that the woman isn't sick, but her daughter likely died of Covid, so she's come to the hospital seeking solace. And now she's experiencing chest pains. I can see that she's medically fine. She's grieving, but she doesn't need to be in the emergency room. Then I gently tell her that what she's going through is trauma and loss. It's not going to go away when she goes home, but it's also not going to get better in the emergency room, where there's a good chance she'll receive additional exposure to the virus.

I finally get to my car, and as I start it up, I brace myself, because now I need to check in with my dad. He's been alone, without my mom, for thirty years, and that means my older sister, an Air Force veteran who lives outside Boston, and I carry a lot of the emotional burden for him. I'm the youngest. My middle sister died after a battle with cancer, and watching her extended struggle and her doctors' valiant efforts to save her life was one of the things that influenced my choice to go into medicine. My parents also lost another child, a girl, at birth.

I've always been willing to support my dad, even if it

means fielding five or six calls from him a day. But it's been harder lately; there's just too much going on. It hurts to tell him that. But he's agreed that instead of his calling me half a dozen times daily, I'll call him at 7:00 P.M. So after every shift, I clean up, get in my car, put him on speakerphone, and head north.

But today I don't have anything to say. The things we've always discussed—parenting advice, politics, articles that he clips and sends to me—have been pushed to the side. I want to unload, but it would be unfair to burden him with my sadness. He's already lost so much. I don't want him to worry about me. So, for the first time in my life, I lie to my father. I tell him everything is fine, because I can't let him know how much I'm struggling, how bad this is, and that the weight of it feels like it might crush me.

When I get home, I begin to call the families of my patients who have died. I've never done this before, but tonight I need to. I need to do something more proactive, more caring, between the sickness and death, and these family members have a right to know what happened to their loved ones—if they want to hear it. That doesn't mean relating the disturbing medical details of how a patient spent their final moments—just the reassurance that they weren't alone. I ask the families to tell me something about the person they lost. Some of them have a story, but mostly they end up instead showing me kindness, which just blows me away. They tell me how thankful they are when I say that their husband or wife or grandmother or son didn't suffer. I realize that I'm glad I'm doing this from home: The people I'm calling don't have to hear the noise of the hospital—the patients asking for help, the whir and chirp of medical machinery—in the background. It's a false sense of comfort, in a way, but maybe the silence gives them a little peace.

Chapter Three

It's the first day of spring, and my first patient of the morning, a sixteen-year-old in labor, is someone we've seen before. She's homeless and struggling with addiction. I saw a notice posted when she went missing awhile back. Now she's here, eight months pregnant. She came in alone. No parent. The expectant father nowhere to be seen. She's probably the one person in the whole ER who isn't afraid of Covid. She's barely heard about it. Thankfully, she tests negative.

We don't deliver a lot of babies in the ER, and this is my first since the pandemic began. People sometimes think that women give birth in the ER every day, but that's really not the case. It happens only a couple of times a year. The last patient who arrived in labor didn't even make it through the entrance. A taxi pulled up with the baby crowning right there in the backseat, the mom in a panic, so I ran outside and delivered the baby kneeling on the asphalt in front of the passenger door.

I spent a full month as an intern learning to deliver babies, but it's not really a favorite part of my job. Some doctors love it, but to me, you're like the guy holding the football for the kicker who is trying to win the Super Bowl with a last-second field goal. If all goes well, you'll probably remain anonymous. But if you drop the snap—if there's a complication—that changes everything.

Even without Covid, this delivery would be high risk. But when that tiny infant grabs her first breath and cries, everything else seems to disappear—the crowding, the sick patients in beds on either side, the beeping of the heart rate monitors and ventilators—and the staff is crying, too. In the midst of so much sickness and death, a healthy baby comes into the world: a glimmer of hope in a sea of pure doom.

The same morning, a mother comes in with her daughter, who also is about to give birth. The daughter goes upstairs to obstetrics, but the mother stays behind. She and her daughter have both tested positive for Covid, and she is terrified. We check her vitals and they're stable, so I ask what she's worried about. She thinks they're both going to die. She's heard that women who test positive for Covid die after delivering their babies, that it's typical of the disease. I've heard that, too, but I don't know if it's true. There's a lot about this virus that has yet to be parsed or remedied, let alone understood.

But the problem of communication is bigger than just rumors like that. Because we can't see our patients clearly or speak clearly to them—the masks muffle everything— the most fundamental part of the doctor-patient relation- ship, the conversation that so often reveals what is going on with the body, is compromised. If you can't see somebody's face and they can't see yours, you're going to have a hard time getting them to open up and tell you what you need to know.

People think that the most important aspect of a doctor visit is the physical examination. That is not true. The physical exam is mostly for show. More than 90 percent of diagnoses are based on what the patient tells you (their medical history) and your observations (the patient's facial expressions, the inflections in their voice, their hand ges- tures). I have been teaching the art of the medical history and physical examination at the Albert Einstein College of Medicine for more than twenty-five years. I try to impress upon everyone who works in the ER to shut up and listen, and the patient will tell them everything they need to know. But now I can barely hear my patients, and I don't have time for more than a brief interaction. The method that is most important in helping us figure out how to get a pa- tient better has been rendered ineffective. What's left? And how do I reassure this woman?

She's sick, her daughter's sick, a baby is being born, but somehow—compared with the girl who gave birth a few hours ago—this one doesn't fill me with hope. Instead, I'm anxious, rattled. I look at this woman, practically begging me to help her, and I feel my assuredness slipping away. Her question is both simple and unanswerable: "How will that baby live without her mother or grandmother?"

I have taught and supervised hundreds of new doctors— eight first-year students and eight second-year students each academic year. I like teaching because I get a shot at molding a med student's clinical career. At the start, I always tell them to forget everything they think they know about medicine and the basic sciences, and to approach each patient as a new acquaintance. I tell them to ask open-ended questions, in plain language, and then listen to the answers.

I also explain to my students that in exchange for helping patients—sometimes saving lives—emergency medicine comes with a lot of benefits, including the ability to disconnect when you're not on duty. But it also can mean difficult schedules. It isn't nine-to-five. There are basically 40 hours a week that are desirable and 128 that aren't. When everyone else is leaving the hospital, emergency room doctors are going in. Overnight shifts are especially brutal. This can be a tremendous strain on our families. According to one study I've read, emergency room doctors are more at risk for burnout, chronic fatigue, and mental health issues than those in any other medical specialty; some studies show we're even more likely to be smokers. We're the only docs routinely in the hospital on Christmas, Thanksgiving, and New Year's Eve. We don't schedule appointments. Our clock is determined by the people coming through our doors and whatever illness, disease, or accident brought them here.

Lately, I've been thinking a lot about Richard Koeppel, my dad's cousin who passed away eight years ago. He ran an emergency room in a small waterfront community and was a brilliant diagnostician. He was authoritative, but more important, he treated everybody who walked into his ER— whether a crewman on a local trawler or someone who'd just moored their yacht—as an equal. He'd spent most of his career working in free clinics, with drug addicts, and as a military doctor. While I was still a resident, he hired me for some day shifts. Because the hospital was in a resort area, almost abandoned in the wintertime, doctors working in the off-season slept in a little cabin, and a bell would ring when an ambulance approached. I saw pretty much everything there: heart attacks, car crashes, fishing boat crew members with big hooks stuck in various parts of their bodies. I loved being the equivalent of an old-time country doctor, taking care of whatever and whoever came at you. I try to do that at Montefiore, but more and more, technology and business get in the way.

I remember how, early in my training, I met a New York dermatologist who advertised on the subway. He was fabulously wealthy and offered me a job: He'd pay me $10,000 to come in to his clinic on Sundays to pop pimples. It sounded like a great deal. But Richard told me not to do it. "You don't want to be the kind of doctor who looks for easy money," he said. "You want to be the kind of doctor who cares for people in need."

In Richard's ER, the doctors, nurses, attendants, and patients all knew that he cared about them. His demeanor kept them calm, no matter what was happening. Later in my career, I met another physician, E. John Gallagher, who reinforced those attitudes and values; who was also a doctor for all the right reasons. Those ideals are what made me fall in love with medicine.

THE NEXT PATIENT, A FORMER OWNER OF A STRING OF DINERS across the Bronx, is waiting. We've seen him before, for a heart attack, and he's back because he thinks he's having another one. But he doesn't want to be here. His family insisted he come in, and they're with him, even though they're not supposed to be.

He's seen what Covid does, he says, hints of his Greek accent registering despite decades in the United States, and he wants nothing to do with it. When I do the physical exam, I can't find one objective piece of data that indicates he's having a coronary event. His enzymes and EKG are normal, and under a different set of circumstances, I might send him home. But something's wrong. I'm sure of it. His story is clear and convincing: pain, tightness, pressure. He's likely got a coronary blockage. He's got heart disease and a history of heart attacks. Guys like him sometimes don't tell you everything, and you have to push a little harder and understand that they're likely to downplay symptoms. This, I know, is a case where you go with your gut, not the data.

The next step is to be honest. I sit on the side of the bed, look him in the eye, and say, "You've had a heart attack before. You have risks. Your story concerns me, and it doesn't end just because you had a good EKG and enzymes. You need more of a workup and to be seen by a cardiologist. You need to stay in the hospital and possibly get a catheterization."

I repeat what I've told him to his family. I want them on my side. "We need to get a better understanding of what's going on, and then we'll make our move," I say. "But to discharge him now? That would be life-threatening."

He accepts it, says he's not going anywhere. We send him upstairs, and it turns out it was the right thing to do. Later on, Cardiology calls me. "Remember that guy?" they say. "We took him to the cath lab. He had real disease. We stented him."

He tested negative for Covid, but he almost died for fear of it. Now he's good, and that's all that matters. But his case shows another insidious effect of the virus.

No matter the source of the fear, it multiplies when people get into the emergency room and see the chaos Covid has wrought. Patients on ventilators. Maybe somebody who just died. They see what their future looks like, or what they think it will be: intubation, chest compressions, death.

Even colleagues are saying they're afraid to come in for their shifts, and that has never happened in my career. Once, we had a suicidal cop come into the ER waving a gun. He could have turned that gun on us, but even then we weren't afraid. You see everything in the Bronx. Or at least we thought we had.

Andrew Williams is one of our first physicians to get sick. He is, ironically, the fittest doc on staff. This is a guy who competes in triathlons and powerlifting contests around the country. But he's among the earliest to go down, and I saw how it likely happened. He works nights, and I start at seven in the morning. I'd gotten in early that day, like I always do. It gives the night-shift docs a little break. I was his official replacement for the morning, so he was signing out to me.

I saw him bagging a patient. This procedure, which was not done nearly as often in the ER prior to Covid as it is now, involves manually squeezing oxygen into a patient's lungs once the patient has been intubated and until a mechanical ventilator can be attached to the intubation tube. Since Covid, bagging for extended periods of time has become commonplace, either because a vent isn't ready or there's no respiratory therapist available, but it carries a tremendous risk of exposure. That morning, I grabbed the bag that Andrew had been using to squeeze oxygen into the patient's lungs and asked him how long he'd been at it. He said at least fifteen minutes. This is the kind of encounter we all fear, but sometimes it is unavoidable, and now he's sick. I got lucky, because a respiratory therapist showed up almost immediately to take over for me, so my exposure was comparatively brief.

Andrew has been out for over a week. He's alone, because he sent his wife and newborn child away out of fear he might infect them. At one point, he called me in the middle of the night, short of breath, and sent a picture of his pulse oximeter, with a reading of 92 percent. I called my friends in Facilities—the ones who get things done at the hospital, who know where the moving parts are and how to move them—and one of them drove an oxygen tank over to him.

A FORMER PATIENT OF MINE, A PSYCHOTHERAPIST, THINKS ER doctors live in denial, that it would be impossible to see what we see and not have it take a toll. I don't agree. I think we are, in fact, a well-adjusted group, even with all the risks and drawbacks. We got into emergency medicine knowing it's a profession that's often sad and sometimes tragic, but we each develop our own coping mechanisms. Sometimes that means a lot of compartmentalizing.

Now there's another layer of fear, another threat facing ER doctors, who are always balancing denial and self-confidence—or even hubris—in order to shield ourselves from the risks we're taking. We're beginning to understand that Covid has neurological effects; it can influence your mood or your ability to think, causing encephalopathy (brain inflammation) or brain cell death via oxygen starvation, both of which can lead to cognitive impairment in the form of psychosis or delirium.

It seems almost inevitable that we're all going to get Covid. So we've begun to play a strange game: We hear that someone has died—it could be a doctor—and immediately we run down the list of comorbidities associated with the disease. Did the person have asthma? Were they overweight? We selfishly hope to hear that they were sick to begin with. And most of them were, but there are outliers, perfectly healthy folks who end up in the ICU.

More and more doctors are getting sick, like James T. Goodrich, who ran our pediatric neurosurgery department for more than thirty years. With his distinctive white hair and beard, you couldn't miss him walking the halls. Everybody knows him because he got Montefiore big headlines when he successfully separated craniopagus (fused at the top of the skull) conjoined twins, first in 2004 and again in 2016. It's a really tough operation, needless to say. In 2004, a round of tests before surgery showed that the amount of brain tissue the babies shared was more than expected. Some advised against the operation. But he went ahead, and sixteen years later, that first set of twins are alive and well. They're going to be twenty next year, the same age as my son.

Nobody knows how Goodrich got sick. He was healthy

and strong and took every precaution. He worked through early March, then fell ill and died, on March 30. His one comorbidity was his age: He was seventy-four. He worked just a few stories up from the ER. When I hear he is dead, I think, *How is that even possible?*

DEB WHITE IS THE MEDICAL DIRECTOR OF THE EMERGENCY department here on the Weiler Campus. It takes a special person to do what she does. I was offered the equivalent job on Montefiore's Moses Campus in 2005 and made the mistake of saying yes. I lasted all of two days attending meetings, doing policy planning, and playing nicey-nice. We still joke about it.

Deb is a star, and she is great at all the stuff I suck at. Deb and I went through our medical residency together in the early 1990s, and because of that we have a special relationship. She was born and raised in the Bronx and has chosen to stay here, although she's brilliant enough to work anywhere she might want to. For years, she was one of the few Black women working as an ER doctor anywhere in the United States. Deb is a great boss: She always has my back, and I always try to have hers.

Deb is a classic Montefiore ER doc: deeply committed to the proper treatment of the hospital's neediest patients. She protects the doctors who work for her, but she puts patient needs first and doesn't mind challenging leadership when she believes hospital protocol is getting in the way of patient care. That's why John Gallagher chose her as director in 2013. Gallagher trained Deb when she was a resident at Jacobi Medical Center, a city hospital right across the street from Montefiore's Einstein Campus. She's told me that she enjoyed her residency in large part because of Gallagher's style. His approach was always personal, treating the patient, not just the medical condition or the disease. She credits Gallagher's mentorship with changing her not just as a doctor but as a person. I know exactly what she means when she says that she's worked every day of the past seven years to make good on the potential for leadership Gallagher saw in her. I feel the same way.

Deb also recognizes—and I'm pretty sure she's right— that few others in the hospital's leadership would have identified a Black woman to lead the emergency department on the Weiler Campus. An astute judge of talent, Gallagher chose her for the qualities she shows every day: She loves what she does, she's great at it, and she works tirelessly for the people of the Bronx.

In the first few weeks of this month, she's been through hell trying to make an overwhelmed emergency room function; managing shifts and sick doctors and staff; rationing equipment and protective gear; and helping dozens of patients, many of whom won't survive. She's in the ER practically 24/7, whether to take a meeting or head up the Covid Zone. She never stops moving.

Deb also never stops thinking. In addition to her medical degree, she has an MBA from George Washington University. In my career, I've never seen anyone more willing to try things, to entertain new ideas, in the spirit of improving patient care. One example is wait times. Most people dread visiting an emergency room not just because they might be *really* sick, but also because they might not be seen for hours. When I was a resident at Jacobi, there used to be a clock that indicated how long the queue to be seen was, and sometimes it showed a wait time as long as ten hours. Emergency room queues have become such a huge issue that facilities are now rated on how quickly they triage, admit, and discharge patients. Billboards along local highways even advertise, in real time, how long somebody is going to have to wait to be seen at a nearby ER.

One thing Deb did right away was simply to eliminate our waiting rooms. Nobody who comes in has to sit and wait to be evaluated. It doesn't matter whether you arrive on foot, in a car, or by ambulance. I'm not saying that there aren't bottlenecks, but most of the time, within minutes, you at least get to talk to a medical professional—a doctor, a physician's assistant, or a nurse—about what has brought you in. I think that's a huge boost for the patients, and I hope that it improves how we're seen not just by our patients but by the entire Bronx community.

But right now, in the spring of 2020, these improvements in patient care and perception can't help the fact that we don't have nearly enough Covid tests for either staff members or patients. That has led some of us to pursue creative acquisition methods. I managed to score twenty-five antibody test kits through a friend of my daughter's. But then I was left with the awful task of figuring out who would get tested and who wouldn't. I tested myself, but I skipped my family and brought the kits to work, testing whomever I could. Colleagues who didn't get a test were upset with me for rationing, but what else could I do? There just weren't enough kits.

But here's what's really unnerving: Everyone who took one of the antibody tests turned out to be negative. Given our level of exposure, you'd think we'd be relieved. Instead, we're disappointed. How can it be that in spite of our obviously intense exposure to this virus, we don't have antibodies? No antibodies means any or all of us could get sick. On the positive side, maybe this means that we're doing a good job with our PPE and the hospital protocols.

I'M TRYING TO KEEP A SEMBLANCE OF REGULAR HOURS, TO space out my shifts and work every three or four days rather than back-to-back. In a meeting, Deb brings up something we haven't talked about: depression, stress, and suicidal ideation during times of crisis. She says that she's getting more worried about the doctors on our team: whether we're going to start getting sick, whether we're going to start manifesting our own mental health issues, whether the coping mechanisms we've all relied on are going to be up to the task. Friday night really got to her. People were dying all around, and a forty-year-old man sobbed in her arms, begging her not to let him die. He said he had a young kid. She comforted him, but it came at a cost, and she recognizes that some of us might be going through similar experiences.

"So I'm just checking in," Deb says, "wanting to make sure you have a chance to talk about your feelings." She pauses before continuing. "I want to encourage each of you to take advantage of the professional health services provided by Montefiore." Her offer is met with a palpable silence. No one is ready to talk about their anxiety, at least not in such a public venue. No one wants to appear weak or to disturb the balance that we all must negotiate internally in order to be fully present, to do the job we were trained to do.

My dad has a saying, "Grief is indivisible," meaning that even if you could share the feeling, it wouldn't reduce what you feel. Right now, it seems like the same thing is happening with our collective anxiety. All of us are resigned to probably getting sick at some point, and we are all dealing with death every day. We're all trying to find ways to handle both. Deb called the meeting so that we could talk things through, but no one has anything to say.

Chapter Four

My friend and colleague Angelo Baccellieri and I share a lot, especially that we're both ER doctors who lost a parent in a tragic and unexpected way. (I have three Angelos in my life. If you work in the Bronx, you're likely to know multiple Angelos and Marios and Tonys.)

One rainy evening, early in Angelo's time at Montefiore, he got a call from his mother, and she was screaming. Apparently, water had been dripping into the living room of his parents' house through a skylight. His father went up on the roof with a tarp, put his hand on the edge of the skylight to steady himself, and it gave way. He fell twelve feet onto the ground, landing on his head.

Angelo didn't know if his mother was just being dramatic, but since he lived only a half mile away, he rushed to his parents' home. His father was lying on the ground with blood coming out of his mouth and ears. He was able to talk, but he wasn't making any sense. Angelo called 911. When the ambulance arrived, the EMTs put his dad in the back. They wanted to take him to New Rochelle, but Angelo insisted they take him to Jacobi Medical Center, because it's a true Level I Trauma Center. He called ahead to say that his father was coming in, and he rode along, trying to stabilize his father's neck. The driver, who was used to taking patients to a different hospital, got lost. His father stopped breathing. Angelo started doing chest compressions. He was panicking. His father's heart started beating again, but then it stopped. He fell at 5:00 P.M. He was dead at 10:00.

Like my mother's death, it happened suddenly. There was no way to have known what was coming. We connected over having lost a parent that way. We were both stripped of our chance to say goodbye. That's one way we both identify with those who have lost a loved one to Covid.

Angelo has one positive memory from that night, a memory that moves him to this day: When the ambulance arrived at Jacobi, where he'd trained and still worked the occasional shift, there must have been fifty people waiting outside for the ambulance to arrive: attendings, trauma surgeons, nurses, and others.

.   .   .

LIKE ME, ANGELO PUSHES HIMSELF HARD. HE ALWAYS WANTS to win, and with patients, that means winning by providing the best care. His sideline practice in antiaging medicine is thriving, fueled by his belief that doctors should get ahead of disease and help people live longer, better lives.

Mountain biking has been my sport for more than twenty years, and it's also Angelo's passion. When we're both off work, we'll often visit Graham Hills Park, just twelve minutes from my house, which has a network of mountain biking trails. There are a couple of big climbs that are so hard, they take my breath away. When I'm struggling to get up those slopes, I can't think about anything else. Lately, I've been going there every day I'm not at the hospital. One afternoon when I couldn't get my mind off work, I rode to the top of the mountain eight times.

When Angelo and I ride together, we compete. Those people who say mountain biking isn't a race? Bullshit. It's a race, and we go as hard as we can. While we're riding, we don't stop to talk, but when we're finished we do. There's a place called Meditation Rock that overlooks a big ravine. Before Covid, it was just a landmark, the end point of a typical ride. But during the pandemic, I have started using it for what its name suggests—if you consider crying a form of meditation. Because that's what I've been doing there, more often than not.

On a recent ride, Angelo and I were there with our friend and colleague Dave Zybert, a nurse practitioner at

Weiler, and Dave's dog, Luke. I might have just been tired, but Dave and Angelo were way ahead, and Luke was following me. But at some point the dog must have realized I wasn't Dave, and by the time I got to the top of the hill, he was nowhere to be seen. Dave had to go look for him, and Angelo and I were alone. There was something on his mind, I could tell.

We work with a young doctor named Vinny, who I think has come to respect me and rely on my experience. I like that, but the last shift Vinny and I had worked together—it was Vinny's first time in the Covid Zone—something had been off, and Angelo had noticed.

"Vinny was scared," Angelo said. "And he was looking to you for confidence."

What I remembered was that Vinny had sat down next to me and asked, "How does it work here?" I told him that it was chaotic and that there were always big unknowns. I said that we were still learning how the disease was transmitted, which medicines worked, what gear to use and how to use it correctly. I told him that we still didn't know the end point. But I didn't give him what he needed, which was reassurance that he was up to the job.

In truth, I'm afraid of getting the virus, of infecting my patients, my colleagues, my wife and kids, and especially my dad. I can feel myself losing sight of the reasons I chose to practice emergency medicine: to save lives and to be able to separate work from everything else in my life. Vinny needed for me to be a rock, to be stable and certain. Instead, I communicated my anxiety to him, and Angelo had seen it.

"You know what you need to do," Angelo said to me that day at the park, and he didn't need to say any more.

Over the past few days, some of the docs from our department and across the Montefiore campuses have taken leave or even retired early. They're scared, and they don't want to be exposed to the virus. I think, *I can't become despondent. If I can't set a good example, do what I'm here for, I might as well check out, too.*

The next time I spoke to Vinny, I apologized. "I didn't give you what you needed that day," I said. He brushed it off, said he was fine. He was probably pissed that Angelo had said anything to me. But I'm glad he did.

ANGELO AND I GREW UP AS DOCTORS DURING TWO OF THE most critical moments in recent medical history: the AIDS epidemic and the aftermath of 9/11. Our initial reaction to Covid-19 was framed by those memories. I went to medical school at Kings County Hospital in Brooklyn, and I was fortunate to do my internship at St. Vincent's Hospital in Greenwich Village. That hospital closed in 2010—it was a valuable piece of real estate that has since been developed into condos—but back then it was ground zero for HIV/AIDS.

Located a few blocks from Christopher Street, a few blocks from the Stonewall Inn—both centers of gay activism—

St. Vincent's probably saw more HIV/AIDS patients than any other hospital in America. It was among the first hospitals in the United States to have a ward dedicated to people suffering from the disease. We didn't know anything about the virus, and a lot of med students and even doctors were understandably scared even to be in the same room as an HIV/AIDS patient. Nobody knew exactly how the disease was transmitted. We only knew that it was a death sentence. I volunteered to draw blood, too young and headstrong to worry about the possible consequences.

After I finished my residency, I was offered a job at Kings County. It was (and is) an intense place—a Level I Trauma Center and still the borough's go-to facility for the really bloody stuff, including penetrating injuries like knife and bullet wounds.

Several years later, John Gallagher recruited me to come to Montefiore. Gallagher has worked hard to transform emergency medicine into a specialty that's more patient focused than any other department in the hospital. He's an intense guy, and he doesn't tolerate docs who see themselves as superior to their patients. I view my job as welcoming people into our emergency room and listening to them before treating them, because that's how Gallagher trained me. When I am conflicted about a case or challenged by another doctor on a diagnosis, or if I feel that a patient is being disrespected, I ask myself, *What would Dr. Gallagher do?*

Being a good doctor happens one patient at a time, by

giving sick and injured people the time and attention they need and deserve. I learned how to do that from Gallagher, who was practicing emergency medicine before it was officially accredited as a specialty. Most people don't know that the field didn't officially emerge until 1979. In New York State, much of the revamping of emergency medicine centered on the work Gallagher did at Jacobi Medical Center and then at Montefiore in the Bronx.

In 1975, a doctor by the name of Bertrand M. Bell ran what was then called "ambulatory care" at the Bronx Municipal Hospital Center. Bell was known as an iconoclast, and even Gallagher has described him as mythic. Bell had a knack for zeroing in on people's strengths, and in Gallagher he recognized the traits that were needed to run his newly envisioned emergency department. Bell tagged Gallagher for that task the year Gallagher was finishing his residency.

Prior to Bell, there was no emergency room as we know it today. Patients coming into the ER were seen by medical and surgical residents who worked in other departments, and those whose ailments didn't match up with a specialty fell between the cracks. The vision of the emergency room conceived of by Bell and continued by Gallagher and several other pioneers focused on filling the gaps between other specialties.

The aim was to build a functional emergency department that addressed the needs of all patients. This would require effective triage to figure out where patients would be best cared for, and it made sense for this process to happen in an emergency department. Bell's vision led to the first federally funded paramedic program in New York State, established after the Federal EMS Systems Act of 1973, and later to the first emergency medicine residency in the state, which was among the earliest programs of its kind in the United States.

Bell pushed not just for emergency medicine to become a true, accredited specialty, but also for emergency room doctors to work reasonable hours. A major case that influenced this development was the death of Libby Zion.

Zion was eighteen years old when, on March 4, 1984, she was admitted to the emergency room at New York Hospital with a fever and agitation. She was given a painkiller but was not seen again by the overworked doctors, who were dealing with massive patient loads, until the next morning. By then, Zion's fever had reached 107 degrees, and she died not long after. Libby's father, Sidney Zion, launched a crusade calling for an investigation into her death. Bell was appointed to a commission that noted that some emergency room doctors were working shifts as long as thirty-six hours and that workweeks stretched to nearly one hundred hours.

"How is it possible," Bell wrote, "for anyone to be functional working a 95-hour week? A bus driver can't do it. A pilot cannot do it. So why should a neophyte doctor do it?" In 1989, New York State limited emergency room doctors to a maximum of twenty-four hours per shift and eighty hours per workweek. Federal regulations soon followed.

Gallagher built on Bell's work by helping to create a system that would help doctors make decisions about patient treatment in the emergency room. From a patient perspective, it made good sense, but the implementation of the new system put the emergency room into conflict with every other discipline in the hospital. Now ER doctors would decide which patients other specialists were going to care for. According to Gallagher, "That was all new to them, and they didn't like that."

Gallagher was born in 1946 in a little town across the river from Harrisburg, Pennsylvania. His dad was the son of a coal miner and a devout Catholic. His mom was not Catholic, but as a condition of their marriage in the Church, their children would be raised Catholic. That requirement was a source of the more-than-uneasy relationship Gallagher has had with the Catholic Church and religion throughout his life. But Gallagher also credits his mother with passing the caring skills he needed to excel in medicine.

Gallagher was an ideal fit for the Bronx. When he arrived there in 1975, the borough had the poorest urban population in the country. Gallagher had come to the Bronx not despite the poverty but because of it. Jacobi Medical Center, then the sole site of the Emergency Medicine Residency Training Program of the Albert Einstein College of Medicine, founded that year, was the perfect proving ground. "It was incredibly hard work—days, and nights, weekends, holidays," he remembers. "It was brutal.

But you saw everything, and you earned your stripes." He had an insatiable curiosity and a desire to know something about every specialty, and he spent time over the next several years on each ward studying them all.

Whereas the old model relied on the hospital's carefully stratified system of multiple interlocking medical and surgical specialties, the new model placed patients first. It focused on providing quality medical care and prioritizing patients' rights. "The implementations of these values might seem obvious, but until then in city hospitals overflowing with patients, it was easy for medical people to say 'There's no real medical problem here,'" Gallagher said. For example, after being bounced among various departments, a homeless patient might be sent to a shelter, which was in essence releasing a sick person to fend for themself on the street. Many of these patients had leg ulcers; they needed food; maybe they were schizophrenic. Alcoholism and drug use were endemic. Not addressing these health issues contributed to the enormous challenge of providing acceptable healthcare in the Bronx.

By collecting and analyzing patient data, emergency room doctors could anticipate how different illnesses and types of trauma played out, what tests would likely be necessary, and how patients needed to be cared for. In 1979, the American Board of Medical Specialties finally acknowledged the discipline as an official field where doctors could provide primary care for patients presenting with illnesses that were still in need of a diagnosis.

The rise of emergency medicine coincided with a narrowing of the focus of other specialties. You couldn't just be a general surgeon anymore; now you had to decide whether you were going into colorectal or vascular surgery, orthopedic surgery or neurosurgery. The same was true in medicine, which produced legions of cardiologists and gastroenterologists, but few primary care physicians and general internists. This concentration of doctors within specialties created an opportunity for emergency medicine doctors to become generalists. And within the New York City public hospital system, where a lot of patients don't have primary care doctors, ER docs filled a need. The probability of having a personal physician, then and now, is inversely proportional to one's socioeconomic status, and since Jacobi Medical Center is part of the NYC public hospital system, it often accommodates people who would not otherwise receive treatment.

What Gallagher fought for sounds simple: an emergency department where people who are sick and scared, and often have limited resources, could be cared for fairly and with dignity. But it wasn't that easy to achieve. He had to challenge the hospital's culture to evolve—and anyone who's worked in a big institution knows how difficult that kind of change can be. Institutions have rules, both spoken and unspoken, built into their functioning. Gallagher transformed care at Jacobi by taking into account not only the hospital's rules and high standards, but also the particular needs of people living in the Bronx.

. . .

WHEN GALLAGHER CALLED ME ABOUT TAKING A JOB AT MONtefiore, I wasn't totally sure I wanted to leave my position at Kings County Hospital. But then I got a sign, and it wasn't ambiguous. I was driving to work through the intersection of Rogers Avenue and Linden Boulevard in Brooklyn one day, when suddenly I heard gunshots, and a guy ran right in front of my car, fell backward onto the hood, and rolled into the street. I jumped out to help him, but a fire truck that happened to be behind me stopped, and the firemen yelled at me to get back in my car and get the hell out of there.

Seeing that kind of bloodshed up close made Gallagher's offer more tempting. At the time, the neighborhood around Kings County felt pretty risky. My wife, Janet, and I were thinking about moving someplace more suburban. That made working in the Bronx—and living in Westchester, just north of the borough—a reasonable option.

What I didn't realize back then was that there's nowhere like the Bronx. I'd never really spent any time there. Even as a huge baseball fan, I'd never been to Yankee Stadium. As a teenager, I went to Yankee games at Shea Stadium, where the Mets used to play, because the Yankees' ballpark in the Bronx was undergoing renovation. And seeing the Bronx as being all about Yankee Stadium? That's a true indicator that you don't understand the Bronx.

Back in the 1990s, the emergency room at Montefiore

was a revolving door. They couldn't keep doctors, and the ones who stayed were old-school guys from the 1960s and 1970s who weren't board certified. (At the time, you didn't need board certification to work in the ER.) Most of those doctors didn't appear to be interested in patients' overall health. The idea was to get them to whatever the next step of their medical treatment might be, not to be an active part of their ongoing care team.

Not long after Gallagher hired me in 1996, he scheduled a retreat for all the doctors working underneath him. Though not particularly tall, Gallagher is wiry and muscular, and intimidating in his resolve. During the retreat, he looked every one of us in the eye and said, "None of you are safe." We'd soon learn what he meant. All of the doctors who didn't focus on the patients, who didn't really want to be there, who didn't understand our role, would soon be gone. In their place, Gallagher hired top doctors in emergency medicine. He made it clear to everyone on the staff that his goal was to build an emergency room that doctors would want to work in. And now, twenty-five years later, they do.

I WAS CLOSING OUT MY FIRST DECADE AS AN EMERGENCY room doctor when I raced downtown with my buddy, an EMT, on September 11, 2001. When we hit upper Manhattan, still miles away from Ground Zero, we reached a checkpoint. When the cops saw our scrubs, they just waved us through. I was expecting lines of bodies, lines of injured people needing help amidst the madness. But by the time we got to the site of the attack, we weren't needed at all. Out of the thousands of people who were trapped when the World Trade Center collapsed, only sixteen were pulled from the rubble alive.

I felt so helpless for the next few weeks as rumors of more bombings circulated and a series of anthrax attacks took place. Our procedures for future emergencies were shaped by all that.

Then, in 2014, there was Ebola. The virus made a lot of headlines, scared a lot of people, but the truth is that Ebola is really hard to transmit. You need direct contact. Sure, we were concerned, but we had protocols in place, and we followed them. I never worried that I'd get infected. There was only one confirmed case in New York City—a doctor who'd returned from treating cases in Africa—and it didn't occur at our hospital.

As much infectious disease training as we did, and as strong as our emergency department was, nothing could have prepared us for Covid-19. It has changed everything about how we operate: We dress differently; we triage differently; and most difficult of all, right now, we treat patients differently. I think Deb White has the right idea: She's in here every day dealing with the sick, doing what she can, learning. The same is true for Angelo and me. We are all trying to prevent it from getting to us. Are we succeeding? I don't know. It's too early to tell.

Chapter Five

My garage has become a warehouse for PPE. The hospital's standard medical supply lines aren't working fast enough. In the first days of Covid, we nearly ran out of masks and were worried about running out of gloves and gowns. In the hospital, our garb is remarkably makeshift: I've taken to wearing a pair of fluorescent pink ski goggles that were donated to us. Others are wearing moon suits, plastic face shields, or old N95 masks with stretched-out elastic. We're piecing it all together, scrambling for protective gear, with some doctors able to get what they need and others stuck with leftover or homemade solutions. Doctors are intubating patients and doing critical lifesaving procedures with a high rate of transmission wearing no masks or reusing them. This doesn't make Montefiore any different from other hospitals in New York, but it's disconcerting. I never thought, with the wonders of modern medicine, I'd have to worry about running out of the most basic supplies.

I've been lucky. Friends have given me masks and gloves. One sent me a full-face respirator, the kind firefighters wear when they rush into burning buildings. It was a nice gesture, but a respirator is almost impossible to wear for any length of time. To lighten the mood in the ER, I went in one morning wearing an antique doctor's mask, one of those long, pointy beaks you see in medieval paintings. Hundreds of years ago, during the black death, doctors would fill the masks with dried flowers, herbs, or spices, the idea being that the scent would ward off the smells of whatever sickness was lingering in the air. At the time, people believed it was these odors that actually caused illness, a belief later disproved by the germ theory.

It might not be the plague, but there *are* eerie similarities between Covid and the Spanish flu epidemic of 1918–19, starting with the way that form of influenza came into the United States undetected, even after it had swept through Europe. A steamship carrying infected passengers docked at the port of Brooklyn, and passengers who should have been quarantined were released into the population after being checked by a doctor. World War I was raging, and the disembarkation of a few sick soldiers in New York also garnered barely any public attention. (The virus may have come to Europe via U.S. soldiers, who spread the disease as they moved around by train and ship; it then likely doubled back to the United States and New York City.) In the same way, I keep thinking about those random reports—mostly from colleagues, sometimes secondhand—of mysterious lung infections just after New Year's 2020. Were they Covid? Some later studies would say probably, but at the time Covid-19 wasn't even on our radar. We might know a lot more about medicine than we did a hundred years ago, but so far we're not doing much better in terms of containment.

Seeing that some doctors were finding ways to get protective equipment and some were not, my friend Mark Fenig, another Montefiore ER doc, thought of a way to supplement the usual supply chain. Mark is from Toronto and got his master's in epidemiology from Yale. He lives on a boat docked in the Hudson River off the Upper West Side of Manhattan. He is thin, and like most of the docs in the emergency room, he likes to keep in shape, maybe because we all see the costs of not doing so every day. He told me that he likes living on the water because he's surrounded by a quiet that stands in stark contrast to the ER. He also enjoys riding his motorcycle up to West Point and out to the tip of Long Island.

Mark came up with the idea to crowdsource PPE a couple weeks ago after we drove down to the East Village with a friend of mine who's with the Yonkers Police Department. We went in his squad car and got a raucous welcome. Folks across the city had been banging pots and pans every night in what started as an impromptu show of gratitude as first responders drove through the neighborhood's narrow one-way streets. We needed a break and wanted to check it out, and it turned out to be just the right way to cut the tension and offset some of our sadness.

Afterward, driving back to Westchester along the Hudson, Mark and I talked about the lack of N95 masks. ("N95" is the official designation for masks that filter at least 95 percent of airborne particles.) So he decided to write a letter asking hospital employees to set aside one hour for every twelve-hour shift to make phone calls, write letters, or get people to donate supplies—anything to help fight Covid. The letter Mark sent went viral, and the New York *Daily News* even ran it as an op-ed. People got industrious, and boxes of supplies started arriving. They have come from all over the world—from as far away as China and Israel, and as close as New Jersey and even right down the block. One woman convinced her friend who runs a factory that makes pouches for musical instruments to pivot to masks and send them to us.

A small craft off the West Seventy-ninth Street Boat Basin isn't the ideal place to store PPE, so Mark listed my address as the drop spot, since I'm fairly close to the hospital and have a big garage. Our house has become a daily stop for FedEx and UPS trucks. And this has led to our doorbell ringing and garage door opening at all hours of the day and night.

My being the neighborhood doctor has paid off in our efforts to find supplies as well. People I've treated for everything from skinned knees to heart attacks have come through with donations—box after box, one containing more than a thousand masks. Pretty soon we're going to need to expand from the garage into the boiler room.

I BECAME A DOCTOR SO I WOULD BE ABLE TO SAY YES TO people when they are in need. Sometimes it means helping patients to the very end. Sometimes it means practicing medicine in situations that aren't exactly like a hospital. For years, I was the official doctor at Southwoods, Bobbi and Matt's summer camp. I've continued to work with the camp as an adviser and via telemedicine now that my kids are too old to attend. I used to love going up there for a few weeks each summer, though, swimming in the lake, playing basketball, being out of range of cellphones. I even loved the camp food.

And I learned a lot from watching the way Scott Ralls, the camp's owner and director, interacted with the kids. He structured each day so that the campers had a combination of activities and downtime. He gave them responsibilities they could manage and praised them when they came through. He was great at what he did.

A couple of years ago, Scott was diagnosed with squamous cell carcinoma of the tonsils. Ear, nose, and throat cancers are debilitating and painful and usually have a bad outcome. Scott leaned hard on me for support, and I became his primary care doctor. He'd call me after appointments with his oncologist, looking to me for answers his oncologist didn't provide or for information about the medicines he was taking. He came to the ER weekly for blood transfusions or intravenous fluids. Scott didn't talk to me just about the cancer. He talked to me about his kids, his wife. Meanwhile, the cancer metastasized from his throat to his lungs and his brain. The chemo began to fail, and so did the radiation.

Scott is one of probably millions of people the pandemic has affected, even though they don't have Covid. He's immunocompromised as a result of his treatment, so he's at high risk. He doesn't know if he should venture out even to see his doctors, so I try to treat him remotely. He texts me a picture of his arm when it gets swollen, or he messages me wanting to know why he is feeling pins and needles in his legs, if he's having a stroke. Generally, his complaints are the results of a combination of side effects of his treatment and symptoms of his disease, and they're usually severe. But he always ends his texts by saying that he doesn't expect a response right away, though I always call back. I tell him he's got to keep fighting through it all. I tell him he's going to survive, because I think that's what he needs to hear.

IT'S A BRIGHT SPRING AFTERNOON, MY DAY OFF, ALMOST THE end of March, and I'm standing at the grill, cooking a beautiful rib eye. Matt has just given me a buzz cut; I'm nearly bald now and have a sore nose with red marks from the masks. Somebody told me that Israeli-made face protection better accommodates big noses. I wonder if we can pull some strings to get some. In the middle of this benign thought, it suddenly hits me: I'm exhausted. My appetite is gone. I don't know whether it's simple fatigue or Covid— but I'm worried.

My wife, Janet, tells me to go to bed, and as soon as I do, I'm asleep. When I wake up, I'm a little out of it. I can hear Janet downstairs, putting sheets on the guest room couch. My gut is a mess. I have diarrhea, as well as an achy body and extreme fatigue. A short time ago, these symptoms might not have made me think Covid. A few weeks ago, we were looking at fever, cough, difficulty breathing. But that's no longer always the case. Now most of the patients I'm seeing have uncontrollable diarrhea.

Janet is worried. She pops her head in to check on me and says she'll spend the night downstairs so that I can self-isolate in the master bedroom. Since we got married in 1994, she and I have never been in the same house and not slept in the same bed; neither of us has ever had to worry about getting the other one sick before today. At some point, I hear the door to the garage open, but I'm too achy and exhausted to move.

It's a rough night. I'm in and out of sleep, my thoughts spinning. At the end of the summer, Bobbi will go off to medical school; in four years, she'll be a doctor. Matt will return to Boston; he'll finish his undergraduate degree in another three years. I have the usual worries about them, but the next morning, for some reason, my thoughts focus on

Harris, one of Matt's best friends, who was diagnosed with a rare cancer called hepatosplenic T-cell lymphoma a couple of years ago and died before the end of high school. His suffering is something I don't like to think about, but sometimes I can't help it. Doing everything I could to support his struggle was the hardest thing I've ever faced as a doctor.

I remember asking Matt, when he and Harris were far too young to worry about college, where Harris was, and Matt said, "He's studying for the SAT!" I was the soccer coach for the team Matt and Harris played on. Harris wasn't a star, and he didn't want to be. He was a defender who never wanted the limelight. He simply played his role with tenacity and intensity.

One thing that Harris loved, and that I loved to do with him, was watch Guy Fieri's *Diners, Drive-Ins and Dives.* We planned a road trip that would follow one of the show's meandering excursions, stringing together the best greasy spoons and truck stops in the Northeast. Of course, we added a few college campus visits to justify the trip, and Harris mapped out the whole journey. His love of food continued even after he was too sick to actually eat.

When Harris got sick, he met with a lot of specialists at Sloan Kettering, and I was with him for every appointment. Harris would sit in on conference calls with experts from around the country. One time, after some scary talk, the experts asked Harris if he had anything to add. He said, "I beat Crohn's; I can beat this."

The day Harris was diagnosed, after sitting with his parents as the cancer specialist laid out the awful details, I called one of the neighborhood moms, Jen Schwartz, and asked if she could invite the boys over that afternoon. It wasn't just that I thought Harris's parents could use the space while they processed the news. I wanted to help the boys have one last normal moment before they found out what was going to happen. It was an afternoon of silliness and sports. I remember watching them and having to turn away as I started crying inconsolably.

I knew that for the rest of Harris's life, people would look at him differently. That's what a fatal diagnosis, especially cancer, does to you. That's one difference between terminal cancer and Covid-19. Covid takes you fast, relatively speaking. There's no culture built around it, no support system. In fact, because Covid patients need to be isolated, they get little support at all. Some people might say it's merciful to go quickly, and cancer can be a drawn-out, hellish experience for sure. But with cancer, at least you're usually not alone.

Harris had a following among the nurses in the hospital. They would buy him gifts and visit him during or after their shifts, even when they weren't responsible for his care. When one of his nurses, Mary Eliza, heard that Harris was in the ICU, she left her station in another part of the hospital just to take care of him. Another, Kimberly, came in on her day off to care for Harris the day he died.

Harris had spent nearly all of the previous five weeks in the ICU, on and off a ventilator, suffering then the way

Covid patients do now. When we got a moment alone together, I asked him if he knew what was coming his way. He said, "Yes."

"Are you okay with it?" I asked.

He said, "Yes."

Normally, I'd say, "You got this." That day, the statement became a question: "You got this?"

His eyes opened wide and Harris said, "Yes."

He didn't know how to quit.

When he died, the entire ninth floor staff experienced so much grief that they had to have a debriefing with psychologists to help them cope. Harris made people feel good about themselves and what they did. He wasn't afraid to tell the nurses that he loved them, and they told him the same.

I was asked to give Harris's eulogy, and I can't adequately describe how hard it was to memorialize, in public, a child who has passed away, whom you've seen grow up. When the day came, I couldn't believe that I was speaking those words at the same place where, just four years earlier, we had celebrated Harris's bar mitzvah. I said how important it was not to define Harris by his disease. Although sickness had dominated Harris's life for nine months, I wanted everyone to think about how we could carry forward who he was throughout his life.

I recited a list of things that Harris had taught me—things that guide me to this day. I know they might sound like clichés, but that they were inspired by a kid who was so brave and so good attests to their basic truth.

Take things in stride.

Don't sweat the small stuff.

Be happy in the moment.

Keep perspective.

Accept what you can't change.

Be strong for those around you and ask yourself how your disposition and reactions affect those around you.

Take on every challenge. Don't run away.

Take ownership of everything that happens in your life. Learn it. Dissect it. Don't be jealous or envious. Be happy for those around you.

Be different. Step outside your comfort zone.

Care about others and not just yourself.

And never, ever, no matter what, quit.

Now it's late morning, and I'm lying alone in bed, watching the sun shift, drifting in and out of sleep, and thinking about what Harris taught me, until I am finally able to focus on my own situation. Janet and I have an arrangement with our friend Angelo Cannarella (yes, another Angelo), who is Montefiore's head contractor. He takes care of all the construction at the hospital, but he's also everybody's therapist. He's that easy to talk to. I'm thinking about him for one simple reason: He's the one Janet and I have chosen, along with his wife, Phyllis, to take care of our kids if anything happens to us. I've seen husbands and wives die of Covid-19, so my fear isn't unreasonable, even if we aren't at the highest level of risk. But I'll admit it: I'm afraid of dying. Janet is afraid of me dying. My kids are, too, and though they're now passing the age where they need parenting, I know Angelo would look after them anyhow.

My fear of the disease is purely emotional. There is no intellect involved. I'm a healthy guy. I'm in good shape. But I have this anxiety when it comes to my health, maybe because of the losses I've experienced in my life. My mom. My sister Debra, who died of Hodgkin's lymphoma after a failed bone marrow transplant when she was twenty-seven. Harris. I feel close to my patients in this moment, having an inkling of what they are going through.

At the end of the day, I call Deb White. I tell her about my symptoms, and she says, "Meyer, you don't have it. You're not going to die." I should believe her, but I go to the hospital for a swab anyway. Eddie Irizarry, another ER doc, jams the swab so far up my nose that we joke we're now married in five states. Four hours later, he calls me: I'm negative. And the next day, I feel better. When I leave my house, it's with a carload of PPE. Bobbi and I stuff every inch of the vehicle with it.

Some of the people who sent supplies have asked us for photos they can post on social media, a sort of product endorsement of their gear and their kindness in donating it. Is it against the rules? I don't know. The way I see it, we have an unspoken agreement: We won't blame the hospital for being caught short on supplies, and they won't blame us for protecting ourselves. When you're in the trenches, fighting to save lives, you do what you need to do. And I'm still fighting.

Chapter Six

I feel physically better, but problems at the hospital have escalated. Outside, a pair of refrigerated trucks are now filled with dead bodies. Inside, I overhear two women in beds next to each other talking what sounds like nonsense. One asks a question, and the other answers with totally unrelated thoughts. They continue on this way. We're seeing more and more how Covid affects patients' mental processes, and we're also beginning to understand that these effects may linger long after they have recovered from other symptoms. Listening to two patients holding a conversation about nothing would strike me as absurd if it wasn't so tragic.

I notice a man in his fifties being wheeled in from the triage tent. He's short of breath, but not too bad. He looks over his shoulder, and I hear him say, very clearly, "Oh, shit.

This is where they take you to die." He starts to say the Our Father, which isn't a surprise: A large number of our patients are deeply religious. What surprises me is that a handful of other sick people join him. I hope the prayers work.

With families and loved ones not being allowed inside the hospital, we as staff have to take up a new role. I've resolved to connect—really connect—with at least one patient per hour. It's a sign of the crisis that I have to actually remind myself to do something I've always considered integral to how I practice medicine. Sometimes I don't have to speak. I just sit and hold a patient's hand. I worry that the last person some of these folks will see or speak with is going to be a stranger in a mask. There has to be a better way.

Talking to these patients reminds me of Baseball Dad, and I find the video on my phone, the one he sent me of his son's batting practice. I watch it again, pleased at how it represents a small slice of what feels like normal life. Then I can't help it. I have to know. So I send him a text: *Hi. This is Dr. Meyer.*

In the minutes that pass without a response, I think, *This is bad. I shouldn't have done this.*

But I've already sent the message. Waiting for a reply, I experience a wild range of emotions: embarrassment at having overstepped my professional bounds; anger at myself for having acted impulsively; the kind of despair you feel when you don't know if someone is alive.

Then a reply: *Hello Dr. Meyer. Hope all is well.*

How to describe the joy I felt? *I'm well,* I texted back. *Thank you. God bless.* I'm not religious. But at that moment, I'm beside myself with gratitude to know that he's survived.

God Bless you, Dr. Meyer. I appreciate everything you have done for me and everyone. You continue to help people. I wish you all the best. You are amazing.

I wish I could say that Baseball Dad's survival is a turning point—I know we still have such a long way to go—but it is, at least, the good news I need, at the time I need it most.

I CAN'T GET USED TO HOW QUICKLY PATIENTS ARE DECLINING, how those who don't seem sick can require intubation in a very short time. I have a patient who came in this morning with an oxygen saturation level of 100 percent. She was talking coherently, and then two hours later she stopped breathing. I had a father and a daughter who came in together. We stabilized the daughter and put the father on supplemental oxygen. No ventilator yet, but he's hanging by a thread. The daughter gets to go home. She doesn't want to, but she has to take care of her mother. Her dad is going to have to face whatever happens on his own.

I watch another refrigerated truck pull up alongside the dock leading into the emergency room. It can hold sixty-one bodies, and I wonder how many people in the Covid Zone will end up in those trucks. I have been thinking a lot about the term "black tag," which is something that is usually reserved for disasters. It refers to a patient who is either deceased or still alive but can't be saved. With a black tag patient, you go against everything you've trained for as a doctor, everything you believe, and you walk away. You let the inevitable take its course so you can work on the patients who can actually be saved, who have a chance of going home.

The younger doctors are still doing CPR for longer than they probably should. Pre-Covid, if a patient's family member was present, they'd become part of the process. They'd see us taking heroic measures, yelling out orders, doing intubations, bringing in respiratory therapists, and they'd know that we'd done all we could. We'd give them the time they needed to process what was happening. But there are no bystanders in the Covid Zone. Nobody gets to say goodbye; nobody sees their mother or father die. We want to save everybody, but we can't. If we're honest and thoughtful, we can save the ones who can be saved.

Ironically, we haven't had to resort to a black tag level of triage, partly because the patients who die often die quickly. But also, perhaps, we're getting better, bit by bit, at understanding this disease. I hope it means improved survival rates. But it's hard to tell right now.

I'M CALLED TO ONE OF OUR SIX NEGATIVE PRESSURE ROOMS. We have three in the Blue Zone and three in the Red Zone. Somebody told me that if we wanted, we could put the whole emergency room under negative pressure. But right now, we're working with what we have. The patient in the room is a fifty-nine-year-old woman. That's all I know. I don't have time to look at her name or where she's from. In twenty minutes, five more patients are rolled in.

I watch as Sean, a patient care technician, tries to move the huge body of a patient who has just died. Sean is a kid, and I call him that not just because he's so young—only twenty-eight—but because he's always enthusiastic and gung ho. He's been working in the ER for five years—drawing blood, performing EKGs—but thanks to Covid-19, a person's job description means nothing. So Sean's present assignment is to move bodies. He has received a field promotion to pallbearer. Sean says he feels a little guilty about admitting this, but he likes this new part of his job. He says it's exciting. After reading the paper, watching the news, seeing what's happening in the world, he comes in to work and feels like he's at the center of the action.

Day after day, Sean moves bodies. The job makes *his* whole body ache—his arms, back, legs. He says he tries to treat the bodies with respect, and I know he does. He's doing the job and doing it well, and I'm proud of him. But the numbers continue to overwhelm. Our morgue is still full, the refrigerated trucks are nearly full, and the funeral homes aren't accepting any more cadavers. The normal routine for getting a dead body from the hospital to burial has been disrupted, and now it feels like the whole system is on the verge of collapse.

Sean curses the funeral homes for allowing the bodies to go to Hart Island, and I pause for a moment, stunned at the mention of the location of New York City's potter's field. That's where we believe my infant sister's body was taken. In the years since my mother's death, this fact has haunted my father, who has asked me if I think my sister's body could somehow be located and moved to be with my mother and my other sister, Debra—and him when he dies. I shudder to think of other families facing a similar dilemma years from now.

Sean says his biggest fear is infecting his family, so he sleeps in the basement, while his parents and grandparents are upstairs. When I ask him if he feels like all of this—the isolation, the sickness, the death—is going to affect him long term, he shrugs, says that he doesn't believe in PTSD. "A couple of beers and I'm good."

But with all the protective gear, you can't tell who's a doctor or nurse and who isn't, and Sean is troubled by this. He makes a confession: A patient who was struggling to breathe managed to get a few words out, and thinking Sean was a doctor, she asked if she was going to live. "Am I going to be okay, Doc?" she asked. He told the patient she was going to be fine. He feels guilty about not correcting her, about allowing her to believe he was a doctor. But I tell him it's okay, that I'm glad he was able to offer some reassurance. It's something all of us should be doing more often.

. . .

A NURSE GETS A CALL THAT HER GRANDMOTHER HAS JUST
died upstate. We all stop what we're doing for the moment
it takes to watch her as she leaves. Then we're back in it.
We're practicing medicine in ways we never practiced it
before. Prior to Covid, no one in the emergency room
wore a gown. Now that the protocol is to wear one, we
should have the yellow, disposable kind that we change between patients. But those more comfortable gowns are long
gone, and the ones we have left are full-body, long-sleeved
gowns made of suffocating vinyl. Hours into a shift, I'm
dizzy with a headache from the carbon dioxide retained by
my mask and dripping with sweat under my gown.

A few years ago, Bobbi and I, along with a couple of her
premed friends, went to Haiti as volunteers on a public
health project with Remote Area Medical (RAM), a char-
ity that provides pop-up clinics in places with few medical
facilities. We offered urgent and basic services for people
who had no healthcare—women prisoners and villagers
living in the countryside. We'd do a quick physical exam,
try to address their concerns, and dispense medicine as necessary. We had dentists to fix teeth, and we helped fit people
with eyeglasses, trying different donated pairs on everyone
who needed them, all trial and error, until we found a pair
that worked. Back then, in Haiti, a country devastated by
earthquakes and diseases like cholera, we had the basics. If
someone came in with high blood pressure, I had medicine
to give them. If they had a rash, they'd get a topical oint-
ment.

Now, in 2020, New York City sometimes feels like it's in worse shape than Haiti after the 2010 earthquake. How could that be? The biggest city in the richest, most powerful nation in the world is on its knees.

A SEVENTY-EIGHT-YEAR-OLD GUY COMES IN, AND HE LOOKS like he is in great shape. He is tall, dressed well: clean white sneakers, corduroy pants, pressed shirt, nice hat. He's made it past triage because the fourth and fifth fingers on his left hand are a little numb, and he's insisting he's having a stroke. I'm almost certain he isn't—this looks like a peripheral nerve issue. In the past, I would have kept him here for some tests, but my sense is that all he really needs is for somebody to tell him he's okay. I reassure him that he doesn't have anything life-threatening going on. He shrugs and nods, and a nurse fills out the discharge papers.

Two hours later, I step outside for some fresh air. Under my mask, the skin on my nose is bleeding. I'm standing there on the ambulance ramp when the guy with the numb fingers shows up again. "You're the doc who sent me home," he says.

"Yes," I say. "What are you still doing here?" I really don't know why he's hanging around. I gesture toward the triage tent, toward the waiting patients, all hooked up to oxygen tanks and IVs. Suddenly he gets it: This hospital, any hospital, isn't a safe place to hang out. Without a word, he takes off running.

.   .   .

COVID IS CHANGING THE WAY EMERGENCY ROOMS OPERATE, and likely how they will operate in the future. One of my medical school buddies works in Boston and is involved in figuring out how to make ERs more efficient and better for patients. But he's also very in tune with the complicated web of hospital finance, and he's worried that all these Covid cases will leave the system irrevocably broken.

"Hospitals work under emergency management systems, but Covid didn't fit the models, so we had to do on-the-fly restructuring," he says. "The biggest thing was that we canceled elective surgeries. This was medically necessary—you don't want somebody coming down with Covid because they came in for a procedure that could have been delayed—and opening those beds allowed us to accommodate more Covid patients."

But he goes on to explain that those surgeries are what keep hospitals solvent. Without them, hospitals are hemorrhaging money. Hospitals will ultimately have to find a way to compensate for all that lost income, and that ties in with bigger-picture emergency room issues, like people waiting too long for a bed. The hope is that this pandemic will be an impetus to change much of what's broken with the system.

AT THE NEXT STAFF MEETING, DEB TELLS US THAT WE NEED to make more changes: "On Monday, two patients passed away, and their beds weren't cleaned for three hours." She adds that living patients aren't being admitted to the hospital—sent upstairs, given rooms, moved out of the emergency room once they're stabilized—fast enough. So we're dealing with a backlog of both the living and the dead.

"How can we turn things around the way we're supposed to?" Deb asks, referring to how quickly we are able to prepare a bed that's just been vacated for the next patient. With Deb, this isn't just a matter of efficiency; it's about respect. Even though we're overwhelmed, we can and must do better.

She recites some statistics: In March, more than forty patients died in our emergency room. More than one hundred were intubated and put on ventilators, and a third of the patients on ventilators died. That sounds bad, but Deb notes that at some other hospitals in New York City, the death rate for patients being intubated is over 90 percent. Right now, we have more than eighty patients who have tested positive for Covid-19. We have the highest death rate and the highest length of stay for patients of any of the Montefiore locations—and this is because our patients have, by far, the most severe comorbidities. We are, indeed, the most overwhelmed hospital.

One of the ways Deb is trying to remedy this is by moving patients to other facilities, to maximize the utilization of beds and doctors across the region. The transfers are done in a Yonkers Police Department emergency medical transport bus, which has space both for wheelchairs and for gurneys carrying the sickest patients. I've never seen anything like it. I watch in awe as the first ride takes place one day at six o'clock in the evening. Deb could designate one of the attendings to ride in the bus, but instead she tells the staff that she'll go alone with the paramedics. One of our nurses, Joseph Duffy, offers to accompany her. He's been on call in the emergency room more than any other nurse in the previous weeks and has seen it all.

A police officer drives the bus while Deb and Duffy ride in back. The best chance for these very sick patients to survive is to get them out of our overfull ER and into an ICU, but they are so sick that anything could happen. There is a very real possibility that some will not survive the trip, and Deb and Duffy need to spread their attention among all twelve to fifteen patients riding in the bus. This means they may not have the resources to do chest compressions if one of the patients stops breathing. Deb tells Duffy, "Anyone who passes on this bus, I'll pronounce them."

She and Duffy make two trips that first night, transporting twenty-five patients, many of them slumped over, gasping, confused. But all of the patients survive the transport. Over the next several days, Deb works nearly around the clock ferrying patients on the emergency transport bus. She will oversee more than five hundred transfers in total. No one dies.

We've run into another problem, caused by the declining supply of sedation medication. Particularly in the chaotic Covid Zone, we don't want intubated patients waking up. Imagine the horror experienced by someone who becomes fully conscious while an endotracheal tube is inserted between their vocal cords. We have rows of patients on ventilators, and all of them require sedation, which must be carefully and constantly monitored. If a patient on a ventilator suddenly becomes alert, their instinctive response is to pull out the endotracheal tube. So hospital staff must constantly patrol the rows of patients, monitoring their level of consciousness.

AFTER DEB'S STAFF MEETING, I'M CALLED OVER TO EXAMINE A 103-year-old woman whose heart rate is racing at 120 beats per minute. Her eighty-year-old son died of Covid last week. She seems coherent but says she doesn't want to live. She's got a DNI/DNR order. When I question her further, she has trouble formulating answers. Like the two women I heard conversing incoherently a few weeks earlier, this patient is confused. She says her daughter is home with Covid, so I get the phone number and call. The daughter tells me that her mother had severe diarrhea the day before, and then the confusion came. This is something we're seeing a lot of, too: It hits the gut, then it hits the brain.

"Can I see my mom?" the daughter asks. "Just fifteen minutes. Can I come in?"

I tell her that we can't allow that.

"Please," she says. "She buried her son just a few days ago."

My heart is breaking, but it's too dangerous. I tell her no again, that we don't have the time to gown her up. She reminds me: "I've already been exposed."

That clinches it. I ask Deb. "Go for it," she says.

Thirty minutes later, the daughter arrives. It's a very public goodbye. No curtains. No barriers. No infection control. No privacy.

But it is a goodbye.

OUR UNDERSTANDING OF COVID IS CHANGING. OR MAYBE A better way to say it is that our misunderstanding is evolving. The process takes me back to my start as a doctor, when we learned by recognizing patterns. In this case, we first recognized Covid by the shortness of breath we call air hunger. Those patients had a fever. Then came the patients with diarrhea and vomiting. Then came the cognitive impairments. Now we're also seeing clotting, which leads to pulmonary embolisms, renal effects, and the need for urgent dialysis.

In the beginning, labs didn't seem necessary; we were treating based on what we saw. But now we've had time to examine X-rays and run lab tests and examine abnormal findings. A "successful" virus, in order to replicate without burning out too fast, doesn't kill its host, or at least not very fast. (This is why Ebola outbreaks, though dramatic, often run their course.) Covid feels like a killer that moves at just the right speed to keep itself going. It is powerful but calculating.

The X-rays are horrific: entire lungs filled with viral pus. Some people say it looks like high-altitude pulmonary edema, but different theories abound. All day long, I'm getting links from various critical care experts with different ideas, although in the end every image comes back with the same reading: viral pneumonia.

The instances of deep vein thrombosis and pulmonary embolisms mean that Covid-19 is causing the blood to coagulate. These clots tend to form in the lower extremities and travel to the lungs, where the real damage occurs and they can sometimes be the cause of death. These are the same kind of clots that can happen on long airplane rides, the reason doctors encourage people to move around and stretch.

Clots likely caused deaths early in the pandemic; we just didn't know about them until we started running tests, like the D-dimer test, a standard test that detects protein fragments in blood. The results indicated that we need to treat all Covid patients with anticoagulation. Hematologists are now recommending that anyone testing positive for Covid should take aspirin or an even stronger blood thinner.

The other thing we're noticing is inflammation. One of the ways to test for inflammation is to look at a marker called C-reactive protein (CRP) in the blood. Angelo Baccellieri and I sometimes test our own levels, and we try to keep the marker at zero, as there's evidence that inflammation can lead to all kinds of chronic medical problems. With Covid, we're seeing inflammation levels in the 20s and even as high as the 40s, levels the average clinician has never seen before.

It's getting so this disease seems to be changing even over the course of a single shift. Most emergency rooms use electronic medical records (EMRs) to document patient encounters and place orders for blood work, medication, and imaging, and it's quite common to see test recommendations or new treatments emerge based on the constant flow of incoming information. Every morning, we get an email detailing ideas on treatment and recommendations from our infectious disease specialists. We're instituting procedures faster than I've ever seen in my career, and it is, in a way, exciting.

During the early part of the crisis, we were indemnified against malpractice suits, so we tried unproven treatments, some of which we now believe are sound (like convalescent plasma, when appropriate) and others that have been discredited (like hydroxychloroquine, the malaria drug whose use unfortunately became a political issue).

But more often than not, it still feels like we don't know nearly enough. We have to hypothesize based on our individual clinical experiences, and that makes for tense medicine. We put patients on ventilators, and some of them die. Rather than repeating the same thing over and over, with death feeling like an inevitable outcome, we think it's reasonable to try something different. But what might that be?

I call a patient's brother and children to discuss a DNI/DNR directive. His daughter says that two years ago, her father said he never wanted to be on a vent. He didn't put it in writing, but his brother says he heard it. But then the patient's son says his father would have wanted to be saved at all costs. When there are diverging opinions within a family, heroic measures take precedence. "We'll do everything we can," I say.

The next time I step outside, I look over toward the condensers that are generating the oxygen for the hospital. They're working so hard that huge chunks of ice have formed around them, and someone has to come out and hose them down every few hours. Beyond them are the refrigerated trucks, the ones used to store bodies. I notice a woman who looks to be about thirty standing nearby.

"My parents are in that truck," she says.

"Is that why you're here?"

"No," she replies. "I think I have Covid."

She has palpitations and an elevated heart rate. But her oxygen saturation is normal. Her breathing is okay. She's going to be sent home, even if she tests positive. "My mother's illness looked like an allergy attack at first," she says. "That's what they told her."

I can't read her tone. Is she angry? Or is she just stating the facts? Does it make a difference? Her parents aren't going to get the memorial they imagined. Even though they have a daughter who cares about them, with funerals so hard to come by, they're likely headed for Hart Island.

We hope that our learning curve, as painful as it is, can benefit others. Later, when I speak to a former intern of mine who's now a doctor with a big healthcare system in the Washington, D.C., area, he tells me that they were seeing cases throughout the early spring, but they were mild enough to send the patients home. "Then, in late April, things started blowing up," he says. "We had huge influxes into our triage tents, and we were suffocating—going from four or five Covid cases a day to ten an hour. I'd call doctors I'd trained with in New York and say, 'What's the low-down, what's the latest?' and we'd learn something—what medicines were working, what weren't. When not to intubate. That lag of three or four weeks was all about learning, and it saved a lot of lives, I think."

JESSE BAER, WHO WAS THE FIRST DOCTOR ON OUR STAFF TO test positive for Covid, is back. He makes an observation, which given the fact that he has been sick, carries extra clout: "When somebody gets wheeled in, it's the most terrifying moment of their life. You look at their face, and you see what fear looks like. They're alone. Nobody offering comfort, nobody saying it's going to be all right. Nobody touching them."

Why haven't I gotten sick? I can't figure it out. A nurse I used to work with died of Covid this week; his wife quickly followed. I took care of him for years after he accidentally stuck himself with a needle and contracted hepatitis C. But he beat it. He beat drug and alcohol addictions, too. He made it through, all the way to retirement. He planned to spend those years fishing, and then Covid took him out.

PRIOR TO COVID, WE PUT PATIENTS ON VENTILATORS BECAUSE that's what worked if their oxygen levels plummeted. If a patient had no other major comorbidities, there was a good chance that the vent was going to save their life, enable them to go home. We thought the same would hold true for Covid-19 pneumonia, but somehow it doesn't: More people than should be are dying on vents. At the same time, it doesn't make sense *not* to ventilate people with blood oxygen levels of 70 or 80 percent. Every single bit of accumulated experience and medical wisdom, all the algorithms that determine best practices in treatment, scream *ventilate*. But it turns out that experience, wisdom, and evidence can sometimes be wrong.

The revelation comes on the Thursday before Easter. A patient is wheeled in. He's got all the risks. He's overweight. He's coughing. He's complaining that he can't breathe. His blood oxygen is 72 percent. We take him to a negative pressure room, where eight of us are working on him at once. His gurney is against a wall, and one of the nurses carries in the heavy yellow case that holds the ventilator. Alongside him are the tools we're going to need to insert the breathing tube: the sedating drugs, the instruments that guide the endotracheal tube. The nurse anesthetist who's been helping us with this is ready. Then something happens.

The guy is talking. Not gasping-for-air talking. He's almost chatting. He's saying he's having trouble breathing, but he's not having trouble *saying* he's having trouble breathing. I can't impress upon you how unusual this is. Blood oxygen of 72 and holding a conversation? That's not supposed to happen. I wish I could say that I was the one who thought of it, but it was one of the other doctors. "Before we intubate, let's try moving this guy," he says.

When a patient isn't breathing well, one of the things we can do is try to roll the patient onto their stomach, because when you're on your back, gravity compresses the lungs and makes it harder to get air. We tell him what we're planning: "We're going to roll you onto your belly," we say, "to see if that helps you breathe. But we're going to need your help."

He's a big guy, and it's no easy task to move him. It takes four of us to slowly turn him onto his stomach; he does his best to assist, letting out pained groans and sighs. But finally, he's no longer on his back. He curls up in a natural, almost fetal, position.

We watch. The pulse oximeter, a little clip attached to his thumb, is connected by a wire to a monitor that gives an instant readout, along with the patient's blood pressure and heart rate. Once the patient is turned, all of us stare in amazement as the blood oxygen percentages tick upward: 75, 80, 85 . . . 90.

He's breathing.

Is the answer that simple?

Up to this point, the protocol said to ventilate. But a lot of patients have died, and after witnessing what just happened, I'm thinking there's going to be a conversation, maybe soon, about changing the protocol. The whole world is talking about ventilators, and this revelation—based on the outcome of this one patient and similar outcomes at other hospitals at about the same time—will spread quickly throughout the medical community.

Our in-house critical care experts start to talk about the turning technique, which is technically called "proning." I happen to hear from a colleague I haven't spoken to in years who works for a large hospital system in northern Virginia. He recently decided to adopt proning after talking to a mutual friend who works at Columbia University Irving Medical Center in Manhattan. The Columbia findings later showed that twelve out of nineteen patients who were turned onto their stomachs didn't require the intubation they might have needed if they'd been left on their backs.

Proning is basic physical medicine. We've known how to do it for a long time. We just weren't connecting the dots. Now that we are, we can save more lives. Deb puts it best when we discuss it later: "This is the most dynamic situation I've ever seen in medicine. We are constantly learning what to do by doing it." We're all sending memos, making calls, reading blogs, trying to learn what we can and then share what we've learned. Should we have known this particular bit of information sooner? I don't know. I'm just grateful that we have a new approach. I make a vow to myself: *I'm not going to intubate anyone with Covid unless there's absolutely no other way to keep that person alive. And even then, I'm going to think long and hard about it.*

THE NEXT DAY, MY SHIFT ENDS AT 3:00 P.M., AND THE WEATHER is bad. Even so, I get into my car and drive out to Queens, to the beach. It's only a few blocks from my dad's house, but I just want to sit by myself. I don't want to be a son or a husband or a father or a doctor today. So I sneak by Dad's house and park down the street. A few steps onto the sand, I run into one of my neighborhood friends, Mike. Back in 1991, his mother was my first death as a licensed doctor when I was an intern at St. Vincent's. She died of cancer. It is so unusual to have contact, as an ER doctor, with the family of a deceased patient, but I see Mike and his father, Jim, all the time. And even after all these years, they thank me for taking care of Lorraine. It always makes me feel so awkward, both because I feel like I failed them and because I feel I am undeserving of their gratitude.

When I see Mike, he is usually sitting on his porch or near the shore or in his yard. We often make small talk. But this time, after a greeting, Mike asks the big question: "How bad is it?"

As soon as he asks, his face falls. He instinctively grasps that this is not the time to talk about it. Usually I decline his offer of a beer, but today I ask for one, and he runs inside his house and brings back two Bud Lights. I sneak back up the street and into my dad's garage and grab a folding chair, setting it up on the sand. Because it's early April and a little chilly, and especially because the entire city is on lockdown, for as far as I can see I'm the only person on the beach in either direction.

I think about how sometime soon, when this pandemic is over, we're going to find out what we neglected to treat while focusing on Covid. We'll see the advanced cancers, the results of undiagnosed cardiac disease. We'll see everything we've stopped seeing. The patients will be sicker than they should be because they didn't get treated. And we'll take care of them. As I'm thinking this, the clouds begin to clear. The rain stops. Blue skies appear.

Then I see them.

A huge pod of dolphins, leaping and playing.

You don't get dolphins like this along the Rockaways in April. Sometimes you don't get them at all. But with no shipping, no power boats, no stray swimmers or Jet Skiers or paddleboarders, there's nothing to scare them off. The dolphins have the shoreline, the sandbars, the channel, all to themselves.

Well, not completely.

I put my beer down and make a run for the water. Fully clothed. And in I go.

It's freezing. It's crazy, maybe. It's amazing.

And as I shiver, I get a sense that my mom is with me. Talking to me.

And suddenly I know: It's going to be okay.

PART II

April 2020

Montefiore has been taking care of New York City's sickest citizens since the late nineteenth century. Following a lavish fund-raising effort by the city's Jewish merchant community, Montefiore was dedicated as a twenty-five-bed "home for chronic invalids" on Manhattan's East Eighty-fourth Street in 1884. It has always focused on those struggling with the most serious maladies, and early on most of the patients suffered from tuberculosis. By the turn of the century, the hospital needed more room and moved north into Harlem. And in 1912, Montefiore ended up in the Bronx, a shift that was prompted by the borough's "open spaces," according to *The New York Times.*

Montefiore largely avoided the 1918–19 flu epidemic not because New York didn't suffer, but because the facility's mission was to house and treat patients with chronic diseases like polio and diabetes. The hospital was able to quarantine while other medical facilities were not. Slowly, Montefiore generalized, adding specialties and eventually becoming the Bronx's largest and most comprehensive health provider.

In some ways, the hospital both grew and suffered with the Bronx. Newspaper clippings from the 1940s and 1950s recount gala benefits, expansions, and expensive equipment purchases. Articles from the 1960s, 1970s, and 1980s indicate a more stuttering growth, mirroring a city and a borough that were struggling with budget cuts and corruption. "Modern" Montefiore's emergence in the 1990s is marked by several milestones, including, in 1996, the professionalization of the hospital's emergency rooms, led by John Gallagher. By the 2000s, Montefiore had expanded to include four major hospitals, six smaller ones, and more than two hundred additional locations. A drive down any of the Bronx's wide avenues today shows its ubiquitous presence, with walk-in clinics and affiliated medical groups dotting dozens of neighborhoods. The Montefiore Health System now serves 1.5 million patients annually.

With Montefiore's steady supply of medical students from the Albert Einstein College of Medicine, the most-modern equipment, and a staff dedicated to community, there was probably no hospital system better equipped for the Covid crisis. And over that first month, as medical facilities around the country shook and shuddered under the burden of the sick and dying, Montefiore slowly found its footing, discovering methods to manage shortages of personal protective equipment; finding ways to free beds and move patients to where they could get the best care; and figuring out how to help medical personnel who were witnessing too much death, too much loss, and were, like their patients, going days without respite, days without seeing their loved ones.

By the end of March, management of Covid-19 was improving, but there was no end in sight for the pandemic and its devastating effects on all aspects of American life. By April 1, more than three million Americans had filed for unemployment. Schools, restaurants, and other businesses were closing. That day, the United States reported 244,610 cases of Covid and 7,924 Covid-related deaths, while Montefiore had more than one thousand Covid cases. The single-day number of hospital admissions peaked in the Bronx at 1,754 on March 30. (Less than one month earlier, on March 8, there were just three Covid patients admitted in the borough.) Covid deaths continue to climb dramatically, with 566 in the Bronx in March and 3,040 in April. U.S. surgeon general Jerome Adams would later say that April would include "the hardest and saddest week of most Americans' lives." At Montefiore, the doctors are about to prove the truth of that statement, as members of their own families, loved ones, and colleagues begin to get sick.

Chapter Seven

We barely made it through March, and now April is here, and the disease is relentless. It is testing everyone, but maybe no one more than Deb White. Before Covid, she spent her weekly clinical hours with patients in the Red Zone, where our sickest patients—those suffering from heart attacks, strokes, sepsis, and other serious ailments and injuries—are treated. But now she spends all her time in the Covid Zone, and she's boosted her weekly clinical duties to near-daily fourteen-hour shifts. She pushes patients on stretchers, swabs them to test for the virus, and takes blood, doing a little bit of everything as a show of support for her team.

Right now, I'm willing to bet that nearly every single person in our profession—especially those in New York— feels isolated by the enormity of the task before us. In an effort to ease this feeling, Deb has increased our once-monthly physician meetings to three times a week, by phone. These 9:00 A.M. conference calls allow us to vent and share ideas and remind us that we're all in this struggle—a struggle unlike anything any of us have ever seen—together. Sometimes we joke around, but other times it gets serious fast, and we realize how much stress we are under.

This hits home when news reaches us that one of our colleagues, who ran the emergency department at NewYork-Presbyterian Hospital, has taken her own life. She was just forty-nine, and the news accounts say that the unrelenting pressure of the pandemic pushed her over the brink. "I couldn't do anything," the doctor told her sister, according to a *New York Times* article. One of our docs who knew her said that she had become more and more depressed as she walked home from work every day, passing the rows of refrigerated trucks filled with bodies. As physicians, we're used to being the ones helping, not asking for help.

IT'S A SATURDAY MORNING, AND DEB HAS JUST FINISHED HER rounds. As soon as she gets home, her mother, Winifred, calls, sounding worried. Deb's father, David, is sick. Deb tells her mom that she's on her way. She drives back down to the Bronx from her home in Westchester with her husband, Al, because her mom has told her that David is in the bathtub and is too weak to get out on his own. By the time she arrives, David has convinced Winifred that there's nothing seriously wrong, that he's only feeling weak and tired. He doesn't want Deb to worry, and he definitely doesn't want to go to the hospital. David allows Al to help him get out of the tub, while Deb stands outside the bathroom and talks to her father through the door. At six feet four, Al is strong, but he still has to tilt his father-in-law back and pull him from the tub as he leans all his weight against Al. Meanwhile, Deb's cousin, who lives nearby, has called for an ambulance. But when the paramedics arrive, David refuses medical care, and his vital signs—including his oxygen level—appear normal.

Deb sees that her father is out of breath after his struggle to emerge from the bathtub. David was a smoker for many years, and his lungs are obstructed, so she offers him an inhaler. The device, typically used in asthma cases, doesn't seem to have any effect. She checks his temperature again, and there's no fever. That's when she sends me a text. She wants to know what the proper procedure is for getting a quick home delivery of an oxygen supply. (She knows that I'm good at working the system.) She asks me if I have prescription blanks, because normally oxygen is something a doctor can write a prescription for. But that would take far too long, so instead I add Ed Pfleging, our senior vice president of facilities, to the message chain. Ed has been with Montefiore for more than three decades, and he's the person who pulls all the different pieces of this huge hospital system together and makes it work. He might have the toughest job in our entire organization. So I ask Ed if he can get an oxygen tank over to Deb's father. Ed's reply: "What's the address?"

Within an hour, David has his oxygen. For the next week, Deb manages her father's care at home, calling him in the morning, again during the day, and once more at night. At this point, there's little reason to suspect that he has Covid. With no fever and with his breathing difficulties explained by a preexisting condition, he doesn't meet the current diagnostic criteria, especially considering that Deb has asked her parents not to leave the house.

David, at eighty-four, still has an active business as a realtor in the Bronx. He and Winifred struggled and sacrificed to help Deb through medical school and her younger sister, Tanya, through law school. If these were normal times, Deb would take off work to manage David's care. But she has a department overflowing with sick patients to run.

Winifred's focus has been on David, but it turns out she isn't feeling well either. I'm on a shift with Deb when her sister calls. The emergency room is too busy for Deb to allow herself to leave, so she and her sister debate whether their mother should be brought in, ultimately deciding against it because of potential exposure to the virus. It turns out her mother has a wet cough and a gastrointestinal bleed, the latter of which is likely related to a preexisting condition. Together we contact one of our colleagues, a GI specialist, and the three of us message back and forth. Finally, the decision is made to wait, and over the next few hours Deb's mother starts to feel better.

On April 4, Deb and her sister visit their parents. It's David's birthday, and they celebrate with ice cream and balloons. The family spends the afternoon and evening together, and though David is noticeably ill, he denies there's anything wrong. Winifred is also feeling weak but seems to improve after eating dinner. As Deb and Tanya leave, they decide that if David isn't feeling better by the next morning, he'll need to go to the hospital. Deb has also pieced together something alarming: Despite what she's requested, her father has left the house twice since the pandemic began, once for a funeral and another time to buy apples. (David often brings apples to Deb, to make sure she eats at least something during her shifts.) And when Deb gets home from the birthday visit, she receives a call from her mother: She's bleeding again. Deb turns her car around and heads back to her parents' home, where she collects Winifred and brings her to the hospital.

It might seem odd that Deb—or me, or any of the other doctors or nurses whom Deb's parents encounter during this process—isn't instantly identifying their symptoms as Covid. But the diagnostic criteria are in constant flux. Up until now, we've treated Covid almost as if it were a form of pneumonia. It's seen mostly as a respiratory illness, often accompanied by a fever. Then we began to hear reports that the disease might also manifest as alterations in a patient's sense of taste or smell. Diarrhea and other gastrointestinal symptoms are identified not long after that, followed by blood clotting and kidney failure. In Deb's case, it makes perfect sense *not* to test her parents. She believes they've been under what she thinks was strict self-isolation; her mother is on a prescribed medication that has gastrointestinal bleeding as a known side effect. Diarrhea, though very serious, could be caused by any of dozens of non-Covid-related conditions. This is how medicine works. Diagnosis is comparing and contrasting, ruling in and ruling out based on established markers, and in the case of Covid, not all the signs are telltale.

There's also the issue of tests. There are just not enough tests available to be able to simply swab and confirm. Even most of our doctors and nurses, ones who've been in the Covid Zone day after day—and that includes Deb—haven't been tested. They're asymptomatic, so why waste a diagnostic tool that's in short supply? Even when we are able to test somebody, the results aren't terribly accurate. We are treating symptoms, and if the symptoms match the protocol, we assume Covid and then take the necessary measures.

Now that Winifred is in the hospital, she receives an official Covid test. The wait for the results almost seems like a respite, but it doesn't last long. Winifred's test comes back positive, and given her age and the presence of internal bleeding, she's sent to the ICU. But there are no beds available, so Winifred is positioned on a gurney in the ER. Deb could probably pull some strings and get her mom a bed in the ICU immediately, but that's not the way she operates.

It's now Sunday, April 5, and David, at home, is beginning to have trouble breathing. Tanya calls Deb for help because David is still hesitant to go to the hospital. Finally, at Deb's urging, David agrees, and the paramedics arrive a few minutes later. They carry David from his bed, placing him on a gurney and into their vehicle. When they pull up at the emergency room doors, Deb is standing inside, waiting with our colleague Mark Fenig. Now that we know David has been exposed, he gets a Covid test, too.

There's a little room right near the entrance to the ER that's a classic example of Deb's outside-the-box thinking. The room has a window, like the one you'd encounter at a fast-food drive-through, and inside there's an array of cameras and microphones. Deb pushed to have this room built during the Ebola crisis of 2016, with the idea that a patient could be put in the room and screened through the window and then isolated and observed remotely, if necessary. Now patients who are clearly afflicted with Covid but not in the most urgent straits are often sent to this room while waiting for a more formal spot in the main ER.

Deb's father is in immediate need, with labored breathing, and Mark asks his boss what she wants him to do. Deb's instant reply: "I'm not the doctor here." She's giving Mark a vote of confidence. Another emergency room director might have pulled rank, but Deb believes that if you trust someone enough to hire them to be responsible for the lives of strangers, you should also trust them with the life of somebody you care deeply about.

And there's no doubt that David's life is at stake. His kidneys are shutting down, so Mark orders emergency dialysis. Then Mark decides to intubate him and admit him to the ICU as soon as a bed becomes available. This all comes without an official Covid diagnosis, as we're still awaiting his test results, and it proves what I've been talking about: We are treating the disease by addressing the symptoms, and both of Deb's parents are very sick right now. That their lab results will ultimately show they are both positive for Covid will be useful—it will put a name on what they are fighting—but having a diagnosis wouldn't change what we are doing for them in these first hours.

ONCE SPACE OPENS UP, DEB'S FATHER AND MOTHER ARE ADmitted to the third-floor ICU, while Deb is working in the Covid Zone. I ask her how David is doing, and she barely stops for a breath before saying, "To be honest, I don't really have time to worry about him." Not all of us know that Deb's parents are here—she's a very private person—but any of us would instantly take extra shifts if Deb wanted a break. Yet Deb knows that the best doctor she can be to her parents is one who trusts that they are receiving the same level of care that Deb herself is dispensing to hundreds of other patients—each of whom is also somebody's mother or father, daughter or son, sister or brother.

The ICU is made up of separate rooms for individual patients, and though Winifred and David are just across the hall from each other, they can't see each other or communicate. Bridging that gap is up to Deb, but the protocols are challenging. Deb has spent the day moving between the Covid Zone and the triage tent, and to see either of her parents, she has to take off the PPE she's wearing; scrub up; and then don a fresh gown, mask, and pair of gloves. Then, to see the other parent, she has to do the same thing all over again. Finally, when that visit is done, she must follow the same protocol before returning to the tent. It takes at least thirty minutes to don and doff three changes of protective gear. Being away from her patients for that much time in a single shift—or multiple times, if she wants to check on her parents more than once—must, to Deb, feel pretty close to unacceptable. Deb knows that her shift is her shift and that her work time is dedicated to the public.

Now that her parents are definitively Covid positive, Deb does have one request: She'd like them to receive remdesivir, a drug that's just beginning to be used in Covid cases. This antiviral has a bit of a checkered reputation. It was originally developed as an Ebola treatment, but it was found not to be as effective as other, cheaper drugs. Early studies have, however, shown that it may shorten the amount of time it takes for a Covid patient to recover.

The word "recover" is key. Because remdesivir is still considered an experimental treatment, the request for its use has to go up the ladder, and later we learn that Deb's request ultimately stalled there. "I had to let that go," Deb tells me. "Maybe the request wasn't approved because my parents were quite old and it was decided that our limited supplies might be better applied to patients with a stronger chance of recovery."

This decision may have been medically sound, even logical, but it must have been very difficult for Deb to accept. Still, when she talks about it later, she's calm, not angry. Her response had a lot to do with her faith. She's a devout Catholic and takes challenges in stride, seeing them as part of a much bigger and likely unfathomable plan. Two decades ago, Deb lost her brother to metastatic cancer. He was just thirty-six years old. What got her family through that loss, she says, was prayer. "My Mom prayed nonstop," she tells me. "And that's where our strength comes from." Now that her mother and father are both ill, she trusts—as they do—that God will be present, no matter the outcome. "It will be what it is," she says.

BIT BY BIT, WE ARE FIGURING OUT HOW TO DO A BETTER JOB of fighting this disease. Small things make a big difference. Each patient used to have a piece of paper taped to the end of their bed with their name on it. We've recently added more information, in big bold letters, so we know who has a DNI/DNR order and who doesn't. We're getting more community support as well. I can't tell you how many pizzas have been delivered free of charge. And slowly supplies of PPE are increasing.

Probably the most meaningful change from March to April is that we're getting more help from colleagues in the medical community. Early on, doctors in other departments wanted to help but didn't know how. Some were scared; some felt they weren't qualified; some just didn't see how they could do shifts in the emergency room without an official mandate. But more and more, our colleagues are volunteering to do *something*. A neurologist I'm friendly with texted me and asked how he could help. I replied that if he wanted just to come in and see that patients are getting enough oxygen, that would be a home run. He said that after so many years in his specialty, he hardly knew what an oxygen tank looked like. So I taught him. The fifteen minutes required to give him a crash course in that specific skill freed up the rest of us to focus on the bigger stuff.

One thing everyone who comes down to the ER from another department has in common is the look on their face when they see the crowding and the suffering for the first time. They're stunned. They all say, "I knew it was bad, but I had no idea how bad." And for a moment, they're afraid, and you can see that, too. But the next thing they say is: "Show me what I need to do."

.   .   .

WHEN DEB WAS EIGHT, HER MOM BECAME ILL AND WAS AD-mitted to the hospital. David was the only one allowed to visit. Deb and her siblings waited for their dad to come home, and when he walked through the door, Deb's brother asked, "What's wrong with Mommy?"

Deb's father couldn't explain what the issue was. He just said, "The doctors said she'll be okay." But when your mother's sick, you want to know what's wrong. So Deb's brother continued to press their dad for details: "Did you ask them to explain?"

"Yes," David answered, "of course I did."

"And?"

"They just said she'll be okay."

What Deb understood from this exchange was that the doctors had incorrectly judged her father as incapable of understanding a medical explanation of his wife's illness. Her brother saw this, too, and it angered him. "You know, we could understand if they'd only try to explain," he said. "And if we can't, we'll find somebody who can."

That night, watching her brother, who was so worried about their mom, and her dad, who was trying so hard to help his wife and take care of his children, and who wasn't getting the answers he needed from the doctors, Deb swore to herself that this would never happen to her family again.

When her mom finally came home and Deb told her how she had wanted to help but could not, Winifred said, "You could become a nurse." But that wasn't what Deb had in mind. "When I take care of someone and they ask me something, I want to explain and not have them feel that because of who they are, I don't think they're capable of understanding what I'm saying," she responded.

Once she became a doctor, Deb gravitated toward the situations where she could provide immediate help and get immediate results. Initially, she wanted to be a trauma surgeon—the kind of doctor who puts bodies that have been badly shattered by external forces, like gunshot wounds or car accidents, back together. One of Deb's academic advisers suggested that she look into emergency medicine instead. "When I did my first rotations," Deb says, "I knew it was for me. The intensity, the excitement, the problem-solving, watching patients get better." Of course, we all know that not every patient gets better, but there's an element of instant gratification in our specialty that you can't find anywhere else in medicine, and I think that's why so many of us absolutely love our jobs.

Each of us has our own way of managing that intensity. Mark Fenig relaxes on his boat and rides his motorcycle. Angelo and I ride mountain bikes. Deb, maybe because she's also a manager, which means she has to be more orderly and scheduled, has her own routine, one that has become especially important during Covid. "I haven't needed to be this regimented since Catholic school," Deb says. Every morning, she gets up and runs on her treadmill for twenty minutes. She likes upbeat music, like Drake or Cardi B. Then, as she drives to work, she listens to morning Mass. Her routine of energy and faith is what has moved her forward in what she says "has felt like a war since the very beginning."

So to see Deb working those long shifts, still managing all the details, big and small, that are required in order to make one of the world's busiest emergency departments operate smoothly, all while both her parents are fighting for their lives . . . it's beyond impressive. This is where Deb belongs, and no matter what happens, we know that she's going to be here, ready and able to lead us. She's unstoppable, and that makes us unstoppable, too.

DAVID HAS GOTTEN PROGRESSIVELY WORSE IN THE TWO DAYS he's been in the hospital. We've seen this in dozens of our Covid patients: rapid decompensation, a term that in medicine means the body's systems begin to collapse. When Deb visits her dad in the ICU, he looks up at her. "Debbie," he says. He's the only person who calls her this, and there's something about the way he says it, the look in his eyes, that tells Deb that her father is dying.

The next day, David's catheter becomes blocked, and the critical care specialists in the ICU don't think it's safe to dialyze him. Deb takes her father's hand and says, "I don't think you're going to last." It's now Tuesday afternoon. Deb calls her sister. Because of visitation restrictions, Tanya hasn't seen her father since he was transported to the hospital on Sunday. "We've got to make a decision," Deb says.

She knows that her sister isn't ready to lose their dad, but Deb believes that he wouldn't want his life prolonged unnecessarily, and he can no longer survive without artificial life support. "We've got to come to an understanding," she says to Tanya.

David is fighting the ventilator, so it's become necessary to paralyze him. The question now is whether to resuscitate him if he codes. Early Tuesday evening, Deb gets another call from the ICU. "You need to get over here," the doctor says. There's no traffic, so Deb makes it from her home to the hospital in half the usual time, and she's at her dad's bedside in less than ten minutes. Tanya can't be there, but Deb connects them on a final video call. It's an inadequate, terrible way to say goodbye, but there's no other option. The life of this kind, hardworking man—who raised a son and two daughters, one who became a doctor and the other a lawyer, both respected and admired by their peers and the community—is a life that's now being prolonged only by the machines that surround him. At 10:00 P.M., Deb tells the attendant to turn the machines off, and slowly the hospital room goes silent. At 10:22, David is pronounced dead.

Deb's mother, Winifred, is still in the ICU. Over the past few days, Deb has tried to explain to her that David isn't doing well, to prepare her for the news she feels sure will come. But deep in the throes of Covid's cognitive fog, Winifred doesn't—can't—understand. *Maybe it's best,* Deb thinks, too tired and upset to return to her mother that evening to break the news of David's passing. Instead, Deb walks through the emergency room on her way out of the hospital and stops to check on the team.

THE NEXT DAY, DEB ARRIVES AT WORK AND SPENDS A MO-ment sitting in her car in the parking lot, composing herself for the onslaught. Her phone rings. It's the hospital's vice president, calling to offer her condolences. "If there's anything I can do . . . ," she says, and it turns out there is. Deb asks, "Please, can you just hold my father in the morgue and not put him on the truck?" She doesn't like to ask for special considerations, but she can't bear to think of her father's body being stored in one of those orange, heavy-duty bags. She's hoping to arrange something that's become increasingly rare in New York City: a proper funeral.

Deb is relieved when the VP agrees to her request, and she heads back to work, repeating to herself, *It will be what it is.* She's continued to live by that credo every day of this pandemic, through every tragic hour, every minute after endless minute. Covid has been life-changing for everyone it touches, doctor or patient. Just weeks ago, when she started to see how this terrible malady might sweep over her emergency department, Deb devised ways to hold her team together. Now Deb has to hold herself together, and the way she will do it is by dedicating her work to the memory of her father. "I would be a weak leader and my father would be very upset," she says, "if I walked away from the team, if I didn't try to set a good example and work hard. He'd feel like he gave his life, and I didn't honor that."

Later that morning, the vice president visits the emergency room and asks for a moment of Deb's time. Repeating her condolences, she says, "We have Nicholas Kristof from *The New York Times* coming today. We need somebody to walk him through the emergency department when he gets here."

The newspaper is interested in covering the Covid pandemic from the perspective of the doctors inside the emergency department. "I don't know that I can do it," Deb says.

Her father has just died; she hasn't slept. Anybody would understand if she refused. Deb already gives more than what seems humanly possible. If she'd asked my opinion, I'd almost certainly have advised her to say no. But as doctors, we're taught to say yes, to help people whenever and wherever we can. That includes patients, family, friends—and reporters. Deb agrees to escort Kristof, along with a video crew and photographers, on their visit to the Covid Zone. She even consents to being interviewed. When I ask her why, she tells me that her request not to put her father in the refrigerated truck was granted. Agreeing to this minor inconvenience is the least she can do, and though the publication later describes her as the emergency department's "general"—that's accurate—what Kristof failed to uncover was that *this* general's father had died just the night before, and that her mother was fighting for her life upstairs. Those of us who are close to Deb and were working in the emergency room knew by then about Deb's loss. But nobody was going to let her grief become a matter of public record. We mourned with her in silence.

DEB AND HER SISTER ARRANGE A MAKESHIFT FUNERAL FOR their father, and they know that they are lucky to be able to do so. The director of the funeral home tells them that their only availability is at 7:30 in the morning, and that the family won't be permitted entry into the cemetery. Deb says that's fine. They can have a church service without the body, then they can drive by the funeral home for a final goodbye.

There's still Deb's mom to worry about: She remains in the hospital, and she recently developed sepsis. *Her* life is in peril as well.

There's something else going on with Deb, which I didn't detect at first. She hasn't been tested for Covid, and she's wondering—with a lingering sense of guilt—if she's somehow responsible for infecting her parents, if she could have been an asymptomatic carrier. That's pretty unlikely, since her husband isn't sick and few of her co-workers have gotten ill, but just as she eased my mind—"Meyer, you don't have it," she said, before insisting that I get tested— I want to do the same for her. So the next time she and I share a shift, I step into her office with Scott Pearlman, associate director of the ER, and tell her that for her own peace of mind, she needs to be tested. I take her hand, stick a needle in her finger, and milk the blood into an antibody kit. And it's exactly as I thought: She's negative. She's never had Covid, so there is no way she could have infected her parents.

David is interred on April 20. Immediately after the service, Deb and her sister agree that their mother needs to leave the hospital. They don't know if she will live, but if she dies, it should be at home. They're going to need some help, so they bring their nephew along, and together they move Winifred from bed to wheelchair to car. When they get home, her grandson lifts her like a baby, carrying her the full forty feet from the driveway to the front door, where he carefully places her in a wall-mounted stairway lift, which transports her to the upstairs bedroom.

The sisters vow they will do whatever is needed to help their mother survive. And with their attention, Winifred begins to rally. It's a full week, though, before she asks about her husband. Deb explains, but it isn't certain that her mother understands. Winifred becomes more clearheaded as the days pass, and finally, in early May, two days before Deb's birthday, Winifred asks again. Deb and Tanya knew this was coming, and for a moment, they hesitate. Then Deb speaks. "He's passed, Mom. He's passed."

Winifred says nothing. Has she understood? Then she asks, disbelieving and confirming at the same time: "He's gone?"

Deb tells her mother again, slowly, quietly explaining the events that have transpired over the past month. And finally, heartbreakingly, her mother understands that the man she was married to for more than sixty years has become another victim of the pandemic.

DEB AND TANYA ARE STILL NURSING WINIFRED BACK TO health when Deb calls me one night. She tells me about a strange series of phone calls she's had with Dr. Gallagher. In one, they were having a routine conversation about a new hire, and Gallagher's answers didn't make sense. He kept repeating himself and then hanging up. This happened three times. "I'm worried he has Covid," she tells me, saying that Gallagher's behavior reminds her of her father, who had similarly disjointed thinking.

I have to consider this. It doesn't sound like Gallagher. But I ask her how she knows something is wrong, and she says, "Trust me, I know." She called me, she says, because she believes I am one of the few people who can get him to agree to be admitted to the hospital. She knows how I feel about him.

I know that if Gallagher is sick with Covid, he would never agree to be put on a ventilator. But if Deb thinks Gallagher needs help, then I have to help. She knows from her daily shifts—and from watching her own father—what death from Covid looks like. She is determined that Gallagher won't suffer that fate.

Chapter Eight

Nurse Joseph Duffy and I always start our shifts at the same time, and he's there as I'm walking in. Any emergency room would be lucky to have an even-tempered nurse like him. But today, he seems particularly cheerful. I say, "What's up with your mood this morning?" Turns out it's his birthday. I'd feel sorry for him having to spend it in the Covid Zone, but he says he doesn't mind being at the hospital, that he'd rather be doing something to help all the people who are suffering here than celebrating at home.

I think we both expect it to be bad, but nothing like what we see when we walk through the hallway—a line of very sick patients from the door all the way to the triage desk. There must be fifteen stretchers and wheelchairs. At the desk, paramedics are jockeying for position, each trying to get their patient seen next so they can leave and bring in another one. We hear: "No, this guy needs to go first; he's not breathing correctly." "Neither is this one, and she's been waiting." "Everyone's waiting."

An older woman being wheeled inside grabs Duffy's arm and says pleadingly, "I'm not ready to die."

"It's okay, ma'am," he tells her. Then he puts his hands lightly on her shoulders. "You're going to be okay. We're going to take you inside to help you." It's the same kind of response that Sean, the patient care technician, gave that fearful patient he told me about—and then felt a little guilty about because she had mistaken him for a doctor. Like Sean, Duffy asks me, "Is it okay that I said that? I mean, I know I'm not a doctor."

"It's great, Duffy," I tell him. "You did great."

I think it says something about our hospital's culture that all of us understand that our role includes comforting the sick.

A board shows the day's work assignments, and Duffy's name appears under "Covid Zone Leader." As head nurse today, he'll have to figure out how to make space for all of these people. He'll have to move them around so that the ones who need a vent will get priority, and then he'll have to make sure each patient is assigned a nurse.

Four new patients come in; three aren't breathing right. Even with our new emphasis on repositioning patients on their stomachs, some of them will likely end up on vents.

A car pulls up with a woman and her mother. "Please help me," the woman calls. "My mom can't breathe." Duffy checks the patient's oxygen saturation level on the pulse oximeter and gets a reading so low that he's shocked she's still alive. He tells the daughter, "You have to tell your mom goodbye now. She needs to go inside." It hurts him to say this, but he has seen the same scene repeated over and over. He knows many patients with oxygen deprivation like this won't see their loved ones again.

I don't run into Duffy again until early afternoon. Amidst the pandemonium, there's an announcement that more donated pizza—this is New York, after all—is being served in the staff lounge. It's a point of contention whether we should gather in the lounge to eat, since it means taking off all our protective gear to do so. Finding a way to consume all the food that is flowing in safely has become a nearly impossible task, and some of us—including me—have decided just to skip the generous bounty altogether.

Duffy is standing outside the lounge, his hand shielding the mouthpiece of his phone. "Yes, thank you. I'm okay. I'm fine," I hear him say, figuring it must be his mom.

Duffy grew up just blocks away from Montefiore, in the house where his parents still live. Before the pandemic, sometimes he'd eat dinner with them, or he'd drop by to visit them on his breaks. Last week when he called them, as he does every day, his father picked up and sounded worried. Duffy's mother had been in bed all day with bouts of vomiting and diarrhea. Duffy knew these symptoms could be a result of Covid. But he also knew it wasn't safe for his mother to come to the emergency room. He was off that day, so he left his apartment in Manhattan and walked from drugstore to drugstore looking for a pulse oximeter that his father could use to register his mother's oxygen saturation levels. After finding one on his fifth try, Duffy rode the train up to the Bronx to deliver it to his dad. Fortunately, his mom's oxygen reading was fine.

But three days later, she still wasn't holding down food. Duffy decided that if the vomiting and diarrhea went on for one more day, he'd have to bring her in. On the fifth day, she started getting better. When she was finally well enough to talk on the phone again, Duffy asked if she knew how she got sick. "I don't know," she said. "I didn't go out except to play my New York Lotto at night, and I had my mask on." Duffy scolded her for going out, the way I scold my dad, the way Deb White warned her parents. What a world where you can't walk down the block to buy a lottery ticket, where you're trapped inside your home for days on end without contact with the outside world. Luckily, Duffy's mom recovered quickly from her symptoms.

The afternoon is a series of nonstop crises. I'm able to stabilize the woman who grabbed Duffy's arm in panic on her way in, but her oxygen levels plummet, and three hours later she's dead. Sean comes to move the body into the hallway for postmortem care, but there's no room. The beeping of alarms continues, but there are none of the usual patient requests for a glass of water or a prepackaged sandwich. Occasionally, someone calls for a bedpan, which means we scramble to erect mobile curtains. They offer a modicum of privacy, which might seem insignificant given that the body of a person who has died might be only a few feet away, but it's the best we can do.

Duffy's shift ends at 7:00 P.M., but because of the work he's doing with Deb on the Yonkers emergency medical transport bus, he's still at the hospital at 10:00. By this time, he's dehydrated and utterly exhausted. His feet throb from being on them all day as he walks to catch the train back to Manhattan. On the way, he phones to check in with his parents. He's late calling, and his mom has been worrying. "Are you okay?" she asks.

"Yes," he says. "I'm okay."

"What did you do today?" she asks, sad not to have seen him on his birthday.

"I had to help get patients to another hospital because we need space," he says, leaving out all the details that make emergency medical transports both traumatic and dangerous.

"Did you eat?" she asks. Every other birthday of his life, she's cooked for him.

"Not yet," he says, thinking how the last thing he had to eat was a slice of pizza in the lounge more than nine hours ago.

"Do you have food?"

"Yes, don't worry about it. I'm okay."

When he gets off the train, he walks down Ninth Avenue to his apartment in Hell's Kitchen. He's used to seeing throngs of people out at this time of night, but since the pandemic struck, the streets have been empty. He walks up the four flights of stairs, gets undressed on the landing outside his door, and puts his scrubs into a bag. These days he's happy to be the only tenant on his floor. From there he goes straight to the shower. Too tired to think about food, he pulls leftovers out of the refrigerator, and they're still on the counter when he collapses across his bed.

Duffy is off the next day, and the sun is just rising when he wakes in a panic. Maybe he's dreaming, but he can't get a breath of air, and he thinks, *Who's going to help me? I'm the only one on the fourth floor.* Not knowing what else to do, he runs down the four flights of stairs that lead out of his apartment building, wearing his slippers and the T-shirt and sweatpants he slept in. He's scared because he knows the long wait time before getting admitted to the hospital. He's pretty sure he'll need to be put on a ventilator. So here he is, standing alone on Ninth Avenue, since the only solution he can think of is to get outside into the open air.

He forces himself to concentrate on his breathing. When he starts to feel a little better, he tells himself, *You're okay. You're having a little bit of a panic attack.* And indeed that's all it is. He talks himself down. His birthday behind him, he's made it to a new year.

DUFFY IS GOING TO BE OKAY, AND SO IS HIS MOM, BUT JOHN Gallagher may not be. Gallagher manages three large emergency rooms and a couple of smaller ones within the system. In the earliest days of the pandemic, this means talking to the directors in each emergency room every day, and when an ER is overwhelmed, Gallagher arranges for the transport to move patients within the Montefiore system. He pushes on, giving up sleep, working nearly nonstop until the afternoon a member of his staff stops him and says, "Look, we don't want you in here. If you're going to run this thing, do it from home."

Gallagher doesn't argue. Just weeks from his retirement, he knows he's in the age-group where Covid causes complications that often lead to death. He also has an ongoing health problem that has compromised his immune system. His colleagues are right to caution him. He can do what he's doing from his home office, so he goes to his apartment in the Bronx. The day he goes home, he feels good knowing that most of the hardest work of moving patients has already been done. His task now is just a matter of making phone calls to facilitate transport for the patients that remain.

Gallagher had a potential exposure. In March, he stopped to help a neighbor who had fallen down and likely broken her hip. A small crowd gathered, and there may have been somebody there who was infected. Now, a few weeks later, Gallagher examines his own symptoms, which have recently developed, and he isn't sure what to think. There isn't a doctor or nurse on Montefiore's staff who hasn't coughed or had a headache over the past several weeks and thought, *I've got it*. He doesn't think of using one of the precious few Covid tests, because things don't seem that bad. Besides, he's at home, which feels like the safest place to be.

Chapter Nine

In his 2014 book, *Being Mortal: Medicine and What Matters in the End,* Dr. Atul Gawande writes, "For a clinician, nothing is more threatening to who you think you are than a patient with a problem you cannot solve." Less than a month ago, I was the clinician in the emergency room whom my patients and colleagues counted on to save lives. I thought I was a pretty good doctor. I prided myself on being responsible and compassionate. But now I am overwhelmed by the number of patients whose lives I cannot save. I trained for a moment like this, but I've never experienced it before. The sheer volume of patients. The intensity. How truly sick people are. It's patient after patient. All day. The same thing, often with the same result: The patient dies.

What is it they say? Doing the same thing over and over

and expecting different results is the definition of insanity? I am not insane, but I don't know what else to do except the same thing. Maybe, instead of insane, I am hopeful. I want my patients to live. But every day, I am filled with a deep sense that things are not going to turn out well.

My friend and fellow ER doc Kristen Schimmrich says she's been feeling that same loss of hope and that it's likely similar for every member of our team. And it's not just the doctors. It's the pre-hospitalization staff, known as emergency medical services or first responders; the nurses; the patient care technicians. In so many ways, we try to band together and support one another. We elbow-bump in the corridor. We attempt to smile at one another. You can't see this through the mask, but you know it's there from the wrinkle lines that highlight the eyes. Still, we are so isolated. At work, we are separated from our patients and from one another by layers of protective gear. We sweat through our clothes. We are dehydrated and sleep deprived. At home, we don't want to worry our families by telling them what we're going through at work.

Even so, Kristen radiates the positive. Before Covid, she worked in the Red Zone, the critical care area where the sickest of the sick are treated and where Deb did her clinical hours. Like Deb, Kristen switched into the Covid Zone in late March. I admire her upbeat attitude. She's ever more physically fit than most of her emergency room colleagues (who generally work out a lot), and that's amusing, considering that she's the one who often declares we're ordering breakfast—then lunch, then dinner. She often brings in baked goods to share. Her husband was recently furloughed from his job, and she has two teenage kids, one with special needs. Yet I never hear a negative word from her.

I'm surprised at her response when I ask how she does it. "I don't feel positive at all," she says. It turns out she's one of the few doctors who has taken the hospital up on its offer of talk therapy. Referring to how the team sat in silence when Deb brought up this idea, Kristen says, "I'm not like the other doctors who have the attitude *We can get through this; we don't need help.* I know I can't get through this alone."

I've never before felt a need to talk to a psychologist, but I set up an appointment and agree to correspond with a therapist by email. The person assigned to me, Simon Rego, is great. He accepts my terms as "rules of engagement," as he calls them, and he responds to my emails within two minutes. The one time, a few weeks later, he doesn't get back to me right away, I'm deeply concerned that Covid-19 has taken him out. How ironic that the very person assigned to help me with my anxiety sends me into a panic when he doesn't respond. Maybe I'm more reliant on my interactions with him than I realize. Luckily and to my relief, he replies before fear can really set in.

I'm touched by what Kristen tells me about her routine when she gets home from work: "I come home from shifts, and the first thing I do is go in the bathroom and strip off all my clothes and get in the shower. I need to wash up, but more than that, I need to get *clean.* I worry that the sickness has permeated my skin, so I run the water as hot as I can stand it and scrub. As the water runs over me, I cry. I chose not to quarantine away from my family. My boys are still young. It would be too hard on them, and hard for me. We're careful. Hopefully, we won't get sick."

She has trouble sleeping. When she can't sleep, she looks up Covid information on her phone until she is so tired that she dozes off with the phone in her hand. She has nightmares in which she's surrounded by dying patients. She is always worried about getting sick, about transmitting Covid to her husband, her kids, her mother. So the cycle continues: come home, undress, shower, cry, try to sleep, search for information on Covid, have nightmares.

"I'm not a religious person, but I pray," Kristen says. "For the safety of my family and my colleagues. I pray that there will be a bubble around us so that we don't bring Covid home to our families and loved ones. I pray that the patients who come in won't be so sick that their bodies can't respond to our efforts to save them."

She admits, "I guess I get it out of my system by the time I get to work." Then she says, "I learned that bravery doesn't mean that you're fearless. Bravery is when you're scared and yet you get up and do what you need to do. That's stayed with me. I try to be brave every day. We've been preparing for something like this our whole lives. If we don't show up, who's going to take care of all the sick people?"

I'm reminded of the day one of my colleagues who had

a newborn at home realized he could smell through his N95 mask. You're not supposed to be able to detect odors through an N95, and he was concerned that he'd bring Covid home with him. It's something all of us are terrified of. He said he needed a break, and that was fine with us. We're a family in the ER; we take care of one another.

"But what about the people who don't show up at all?" I ask Kristen.

"I can't blame them, Rob," she says. "It's really scary."

ANOTHER PERSON WHOM I FEEL ESPECIALLY CONNECTED TO, and whom I confide in, is my colleague Laureta Lahu. She remembers how, at the beginning of March, the CDC said N95 masks were not needed unless a medical worker tested positive for Covid. She remembers doing CPR without an N95. Then a week later, N95s were mandatory. Back then, the rules kept changing. (They still do.) We didn't know how to take care of patients. We didn't know how to keep ourselves safe.

As a patient care technician working toward her registered nursing degree, Laureta sometimes asks me medical questions or tells me what she's learning. She observes that patients are suffering not just from the disease but also from the loss of social interaction that fear of the disease has brought. She says this reminds her of Harry Harlow's studies on rhesus monkeys back in the 1950s, which tested the effects of lack of maternal contact on newborns, showing how the need for physical interaction is as essential to life as air and food. The monkeys suffered; half of the newborns in Harlow's first study failed to thrive. These findings were later replicated in humans. So many people are being deprived of intimate connections right now. What will the consequences be?

"I walk down the sidewalk in my scrubs, and people cross to the other side of the street," Laureta says. "I can't see my family or friends. I'm like a walking freak show. No one wants to see me. Thank God I work with my mom, so at least I can see her. If my mother didn't work in the hospital with me, I would see no one."

Laureta and Duffy are both at least a generation younger than me and most of the doctors who work in the emergency room. Up until now, they didn't see the need to separate life from work. Another month passes before Duffy, who's been self-isolating when he's not working, can see his parents again. He still doesn't set foot in their house and visits instead from the backyard, at a distance. "I go to Starbucks on my break and get them goodies. I hand them a bag over the garden wall and tell them, 'Take [the goodies] out, then throw the bag away and wash your hands.' This is what you have to go through."

Laureta says she's stopped bringing her work home, as a way of protecting herself. "Not doing that," she says, "would mean going crazy."

It's a struggle to try to build in some professional distance, especially when you once saw keeping things personal as a strength. "When those double doors swing open, you enter the Twilight Zone," Laureta says. "You're no longer on earth. Instead, [you're] on a spaceship from a different world. Patients stacked against the walls, all with their heads drooping, turned to the side, their mouths open. They look exhausted, like someone has taken the life out of them, their stares completely blank. Up close you can see them trying to breathe, and you realize why they look the way they do. They have no energy left. They have a pulse, but they're lifeless. That energy, or [rather, the] lack of it, goes into us. And even though we are the ones running around, trying to save the lives of patients who look like they [are] no longer living, after a while, we feel lifeless."

Laureta continues. "In nursing school, they drill you about the ABCs: Airway. Breathing. Circulation. When a patient is struggling, you check these things first. But in the Covid emergency room, everybody needs oxygen treatment. Half of them are so sick they can't speak. Half of them can't move. After a while, you know what someone wants or what they are trying to say because of the look in their eyes. It's like learning a new language with your sight.

"These days are for the most part filled with an overwhelming sense of hopelessness that comes from fighting against more of the same—more death than life. That's why we turn to each other, because after a while it seems like we're the people that need saving, and we're the only people who understand that about each other. We protect our families, our friends, our loved ones from what we see because life has turned stranger than fiction, but unlike a good book, you can't put it aside, you're trapped inside it."

Covid-19 is, for Laureta, her coming of age. The world has infringed on her idealism in an irrevocable way.

I'M OUT FOR A WALK WITH MY WIFE, JANET. IT'S A COOL spring evening, and normally you wouldn't see many people outside in our neighborhood. Dog walkers, yes, but people out for a stroll? Not so much. But there's not much else to do during a pandemic, so everybody's out and about. I'm not very patient on walks like this, so I'm bouncing a pink rubber ball as we make our way home. That's when I get the call from Deb. She hasn't seen John Gallagher since he was sent home a few weeks ago, but based on their phone conversations, she's convinced he has Covid.

At first I wonder if she's being overly dramatic. All we're seeing in the ER right now is Covid, and we think every cough or sneeze is likely a result of it. But given Deb's personal experience with the virus—and given that every time I've questioned her on a diagnosis in the past twenty-five years, she's turned out to be right—I'm then almost immediately alarmed.

It's common for me to ask myself, *What would Dr. Gallagher do?* But now I'm thinking, *What would Dr. Gallagher do for Dr. Gallagher?*

As soon as we get home, I text Gallagher. Despite our

close professional relationship, our social interactions are infrequent. I message him once in a while to see if he wants to meet for a drink at An Beal Bocht Cafe, an Irish pub not far from the hospital. We do this maybe five times a year, especially on open mic night when the traditional musicians come out. Angelo Baccellieri usually tags along. I figure I can use that pretense—to meet up for a drink—to find out what's going on.

Hey. Socially distant drink? One from ten feet apart? Just one?

His reply comes within minutes: *Sorry. Can't. Too sick.*

I text back: *Can't drop too sick on me. You know me better than that. What can I do? Where are you?*

DNI/DNR, he texts. *Do nothing.*

I read the text exchange to Janet, and we discuss what my next move should be. One instinct that has never failed me is simply to be where I think I am needed. This instinct is in keeping with what Gallagher taught me, which is never to make a clinical decision without seeing the patient. I can also say that when I haven't followed this advice, when I have chosen not to see a patient, I've more often than not made a mistake. (Like the time I diagnosed my friend Charles over the phone, mistaking his rash, sight unseen, for MRSA, a scary antibiotic-resistant bacterium that can cause a potentially deadly infection. It turned out he had Lyme disease, which luckily is usually treatable with antibiotics.)

So my decision is made. I tell Bobbi and Matt what's

going on, and with their help I load up the car with supplies to treat Gallagher at his apartment in Riverdale, a
neighborhood in the Bronx. Driving away, I see Bobbi in
my rearview mirror, standing in the cul-de-sac. In typical
traffic, the drive would take thirty minutes or longer, but
during this Covid spring, I'm there in less than ten.

Chapter Ten

As I drive to Gallagher's, I think about what normalcy looks like, and how far we've gotten from it. It is bizarre to be rushing to my boss's home in the middle of a pandemic because he's having a medical emergency.

John Gallagher changed emergency medicine, and now emergency medicine is changing again. Covid is accelerating those changes. The other day, Angelo Baccellieri confided that he misses the way the ER used to be: full of people talking, screaming, complaining. Since Covid, we don't have time for conversation. The patients don't complain so much as confide in us or express their terror. All you hear is the ventilators. We work together in a kind of grim silence, waiting for the next patient, and the one after that. Angelo predicts that we're all going to have what he calls "post-corona stress disorder."

Covid has taken away the most important part of a more traditional way of thinking about medicine: the unfiltered human interactions. That's something that this pandemic has in common with a bigger trend in our business. Nowadays, if you're a doctor in some hospitals or major medical groups, your productivity isn't measured by how well your patients are or how satisfied they are. Instead, everything is calibrated in dollars: how many patients you see in an hour, how many procedures you order, how much you bill. But to Angelo and me, the practice of medicine is about forming relationships. It's why we chose Montefiore.

"I'm thinking about retirement," Angelo said. "I'll give it three years."

I've thought about retiring, too, but never said it out loud.

"Emergency medicine is becoming a young man's field," Angelo said. "Back in the day, you were a doctor. Now a gadget facilitates your relationship with your patient. Technology drives standard of care." Angelo was giving voice to my own fears: of succumbing to Covid or becoming redundant as a physician. But losing him as a colleague would devastate me.

"Before Covid, we'd go to a patient's bedside and shake their hand. That meant something," he said. "It made the patient feel comfortable. Now with Covid, it's the opposite. It would be unethical to offer a patient your hand to shake."

I reminded him of our bike ride, when he was calling

me out on my fear. "You helped me out with Vinny," I tell him. "You showed me I was acting more out of fright than rationality."

"You'd do the same for me," he said. "I know if someone brought something like that to your attention, you'd tell me the same."

Would I? I've been rethinking everything lately, wondering if there might have been other instances where my fear has shown through. Since the start of Covid, I've been so filled with anxiety, worried that I will be judged for the lives I've been unable to save. But trying to nudge Angelo toward optimism restored a belief I thought I'd lost: that medicine is going to be okay, because people are still going to become doctors for the right reasons.

THERE'S A PHOTO OF ME WITH GALLAGHER AT MY DAD'S house. I'm standing in the foreground, eating something with a half grin, and Gallagher is in the background with a stern expression. Underneath the photo, my dad has penciled in a caption: "Alright, Rob, what the fuck did you do now?" That about sums up my relationship with Gallagher. But the thing is, as close as Gallagher and I are, and as many years as he's been my mentor, I've never been inside his apartment in the Bronx. Though his primary residence is in north Westchester County, he keeps the tiny flat in order to have a place close to the hospital, to his students and colleagues, and sometimes he stays there during the week. When we meet up for dinner or a drink, I often drive him home, so I know his address in Riverdale.

When I get there, my first obstacle is the building's doorman. If you're not from New York City, you may not be aware of how much power these gatekeepers wield. A doorman accepts packages and announces guests, acts as a stand-in sitter or pet caregiver, a security guard, a bouncer, a taxi hailer, a snow shoveler. But one thing a doorman can't do is let an unauthorized visitor into the building.

"I'm here to see John Gallagher," I say.

"I'll call him."

The doorman doesn't recognize me—I've only dropped Gallagher off here a few times—and he's not inclined to risk his job.

"Wait." I lean into the desk, ask his name. After he responds, I say, "Steven, you've got a very tough situation on your hands. Either he's not going to answer the phone or he's going to say I can't come up. But I've got to go up there."

Steven hesitates. "I could lose my job," he says.

"It's a matter of life and death," I reply. The doorman, who could have insisted we call an ambulance or the police and is taking a considerable risk, relents.

If Gallagher is really sick with Covid, he's going to need oxygen, fast. I get upstairs and tap out another text message to him: *I'm outside your door.*

No answer.

Don't open it, I text. *Just talk to me. Yell at me. Tell me to go away.*

Nothing.

Does DO NOT INTUBATE/DO NOT RESUSCITATE mean you leave somebody in an obviously desperate state in their apartment to die all alone? I know Gallagher wouldn't allow me to die if the situation were reversed. But do I have an obligation to honor his wishes? Maybe I should tell him I'll bring him a "comfort box," the kit given to terminally ill patients that contains pain relievers, anti-nausea drugs, and medications to ease and slow the breathing. The contents of the comfort box are designed to make death more peaceful, and therefore more likely. But my sense is that it isn't time for that.

I knock on the door.

Nothing.

I knock again.

I hear movement. The door opens, just a bit. John Gallagher—one of the fathers of modern emergency medicine, a stubborn, ethical, brilliant, proud man—is on his knees, crawling. He can barely breathe.

"Get the fuck out of here," he says. "Don't rob me of my dignity. I didn't want anyone to see me like this. I wanted to be left alone. To die."

I'm dumbfounded. He's coughing as he calls me names. Intellectually, I know that lack of oxygen in Covid-19 can cause cognitive problems, but I still don't know how to respond. I stare through the one-inch-wide crack of the open door, speechless. Then I lose it.

"Fuck you! Go fuck yourself!" I scream. "I need to help you just as much for me as for you, and if you're going to quit, then you have to own up to it!" The ferocity of my words shocks me.

For a second, I don't know what else to say. But I realize that I'm here to solve a medical problem. Gallagher needs oxygen. How to get it for him? A standard oxygen tank or two would be inefficient; they'd run out quickly. But there's another, simpler device called an oxygen concentrator that might work. Usually, people have home oxygen concentrators to improve breathing if they have sleep apnea or COPD. The beauty of the device is that it doesn't require an external air supply; rather, it functions as the name suggests, extracting oxygen from the air and delivering it to the patient, usually via a mask or a nasal cannula.

I recall that our neighbor Julie, the mother of Bobbi's best friend, Hannah, owns a portable concentrator that she uses when she travels. She's the same person who helped us secure antibody test kits and N95 masks, so I know she's inclined to help. When I offer to get it, Gallagher doesn't say no, which is somewhat encouraging. So I ask him by text what else he needs.

Coca-Cola, he texts back.

This is a good sign, because it means he's responsive. Gallagher does believe that this particular soft drink is an excellent tool for rehydration. In fact, he co-authored a study on the use of Coke for that purpose in pediatric vomiting and rehydration. But it also means that Gallagher believes he really needs fluids, which means he's in danger.

It's hard to leave him alone like this, dehydrated and suffering from air hunger, but I have to get him what he needs.

I drive home, calling Bobbi along the way, telling her to have that concentrator ready. I ask Matt to buy a half dozen cans of Coke. (Matt thinks I'm losing it, because we *never* have soda in our house.) I remind him to wear a mask as he shops—it's going to be his first time in a supermarket since the pandemic began.

As soon as I get home, everything is ready: the oxygen concentrator; the soda; a gown, a face mask, and gloves. Bobbi wants to come with me, but I can't put her at risk. I barely have time to pause and think about the sacrifice of a friend who is giving up her breathing device. Even though she uses it only when she's traveling or in emergencies, she's making a sacrifice, especially if Covid strikes her. This act of selflessness reminds me that people will act generously when given the opportunity. It's not just doctors and nurses and first responders. It's friends and neighbors, too.

I load the car and head to Gallagher's. This time, the doorman waves me in, and I go upstairs, turning left at the elevator to knock on Gallagher's door.

I have an oxygen concentrator.

No answer.

I begin shouting instructions through the door on how

to use the device. That may seem strange, given that Gallagher has been handling equipment like this for decades, but his mental state is uncertain, and I want to make sure everything is spelled out. He's still as smart as anyone I know, even impaired, but I go over the use of the concentrator several times.

He's still not opening the door, so I leave the Coca-Cola and the concentrator and head back toward the elevator, hoping he'll retrieve them. There's no goodbye. No pleasantries. Nothing. As I drive home, my mind is racing, fixed on a single thought: *Will I ever see John Gallagher alive again?* Leaving him alone was tough, but I had to. He's not going to be saved by just one person. Saving Gallagher—if he can be saved—will have to be a team effort.

Chapter Eleven

When I get home, I call Dave Esses, Deb's counterpart at the Moses Campus. Like Deb and myself, Esses is a Gallagher protégé. Neither of us knows what the other knows, so at first we're sort of dancing around the topic of Gallagher's health. But then we both admit it: Gallagher is now a patient.

"He's got Covid-19," I say, "and we need to deal with it." Dave's silence is palpable, then he confesses that he's had a growing awareness of Gallagher's situation for a couple of days, and it has been really hard trying to figure out what to do. As soon as he tells me this, I feel a great sense of relief because we're now in it together. Dave insists that we call Gallagher's wife, Kathleen, who is also a doctor. With Gallagher staying in the Bronx to keep close to the hospital, and Kathleen at their main residence, we're not even sure

Kathleen knows what's going on. It turns out she had her suspicions and like us was trying to figure out how to manage John's illness and wishes. It'll help to have her on board—she's an amazing clinician with multiple decades of experience and knows better than anyone what makes her husband tick.

After a round of phone calls, the three of us agree to meet at the apartment in the morning. When we get there, there's a new doorman, but we're allowed to go right up since Kathleen, who has sped down from farther upstate, is with us. In the hallway of the twenty-first floor, Kathleen dons her PPE and walks into the apartment, leaving Dave and me to wait outside. Our equipment consists of a pulse oximeter, a stethoscope, and a blood pressure cuff—the bare minimum needed to practice medicine like this.

Kathleen is in there for less than ten minutes, but it feels like hours. Finally, she opens the door and says John is stable, for now. This is great news. The oxygen concentrator and Coca-Cola seem to be working.

As we walk out of the building, Dave tells me that he has to rush back to the hospital because a crew from *60 Minutes* is arriving. Between the *New York Times* article and television spots, Montefiore's dire situation is becoming pretty well known. As he leaves, we decide that John needs a formal Covid-19 test, so I head to the Moses Campus to pick one up. I call Bobbi and Matt and ask them to get more Coke and also chicken broth, which John requested.

When I return to John's apartment, Janet and Bobbi are

with me, and I plead with them to stay in the car, but I know there's no convincing Bobbi. As a future doctor, she's not going to sit on the sidelines. So we go upstairs and deliver the goods. John insists on swabbing himself, going the full six inches deep in each nostril and holding the swabs in place for thirty agonizing seconds. For now, there's nothing else we can do, so I drop the swabs at Moses and head home to try to rest. A few hours later, Dave calls me: Gallagher is positive for Covid.

And that's when I lose it. I take refuge in my car, and hunched over the steering wheel, I cry, certain I haven't done enough. I've never said it, but I love the guy the way I love my father. And though I've been trying to help him, everything I've seen about this pandemic—this awful fucking pandemic—tells me that it isn't enough. Alone, at home, with little more than an oxygen concentrator and a six-pack of Coca-Cola, John Gallagher—one of the most important doctors in the history of emergency medicine, the person who made me, and Deb, and Dave, and Angelo, and the rest of us who we are—is going to die.

I think about his upcoming retirement and how he intended to use it to keep reshaping emergency medicine. I think about his plans to work for a major think tank, the offers he's received from charitable foundations, research organizations. All the good he still has to do.

When Dave and I check in with Kathleen, she tells us that he's reluctant but will probably go to the hospital. She's convinced him through the force of her love and for the sake of their daughters. Dave, Kathleen, and I agree that the goal should be to get him to agree to be placed in the ICU. It feels like we're strong-arming him, but we want to save him. And in the end, it's John who has taught us, first and above all, to be a patient advocate.

I call the hospital's senior vice president, Peter Semczuk, and explain the situation. One of Peter's jobs is to oversee the ambulance fleet, and he assures me that he can have an ambulance at Gallagher's building within minutes. He tells me he's sending it with extra support, including an experienced lieutenant paramedic. I arrive a few seconds before the ambulance, and Kathleen, Dave, and I stand by feeling a bit sorry for the crew, realizing they have no idea who it is they're caring for.

Being taken away in an ambulance is a very public thing, and it is exactly the opposite of what John wants. He's pissed off about it. But at the same time, he is starved for air, so he's fully hooked up to supplemental oxygen and an intravenous line for fluids, wrapped in a blanket, and strapped to the gurney. He doesn't look directly at me as he's loaded inside. Kathleen follows him, and I ask the paramedics to let me close the door, because I keep thinking that this might be the last time I see him alive. I thought I'd have something profound to say, or at least a wisecrack, but instead I freeze. John gets the last word. "I know that look," he says, his eyes piercing me almost angrily, and I close the door.

Dave departs in his own car, and now, outside Gallagher's apartment building, it's quiet. I let my body descend to the curb. It's not long before the tears begin to flow. There in my scrubs, sitting on the curb, I'm inconsolable. That's when I notice that a UPS driver has pulled up, and he sits down next to me.

"Look at my truck," he says, pointing toward the open tailgate after I tell him that an ambulance has just driven off with my mentor. "I'm finishing my route, and not one of those packages is getting delivered."

It turns out the driver has a half dozen nursing homes on his route.

"All those boxes," he tells me, "all those people died alone. There was nobody to say goodbye to them."

Then he says, "I've got my story and you've got yours. And we both just have to keep going."

I watch the driver walk back to his truck. Covid-19 is breaking so many hearts, destroying so many families, but this is no time for self-pity. Doctors, doormen, delivery drivers—we've all got our jobs to do. And we all have a story when it comes to this pandemic.

I HAVE TO UPDATE DEB. I KNOW HOW MUCH GALLAGHER means to her. Later, our colleague Scott Pearlman tells me that she cried after we spoke, and I'm shocked to hear that. She's usually as stoic as they come, and she didn't even cry, at least not in front of any of us, when her own father died.

Deb asks me to cross the borough to pick her up and take her to see John. We drive over to Montefiore's Moses

Campus in silence. Deb really wanted John to be in Weiler's ICU, so she could take care of him. She feels she's learned a lot from her father's death and thought that knowledge would help John have a better outcome. But distance matters in medicine, and Moses is just five minutes from Riverdale.

One thing I've learned from my twenty-five years in the ER is that you can't really understand a person's thought process when they're sick. As a doctor, you can prescribe treatment and try to figure out what's going on inside a patient, but you're outside of that very personal, internal experience. Gallagher, who is a complex thinker to start with, and who has more medical knowledge in his head than all of us put together, is especially challenging, given Covid's impact on cognition.

Gallagher has allowed us to admit him to the ICU, but the second he gets in, he wants out. His reason, it turns out, is that he can't bear the humiliation caused by his intense diarrhea. He doesn't want a nurse to have to clean him up, and it's probably made worse by the fact that everybody there knows him; he can't retreat into the anonymity that other patients are allowed. As sick as he is, he'd rather die at home than crap his pants in the hospital.

Deb, Kathleen, Dave, and I meet at Moses. We try to talk Gallagher out of leaving, but he threatens to self-discharge against medical advice. There's nothing we can do to get him to stay. And despite the fact that we think he's impaired, his words come out as sensible. He's not yelling and screaming and bolting for the door. It's his right not to be treated.

I'm also keenly aware that being in the hospital doesn't necessarily save one's life. The most we could do for him is intubate, but John has made it clear he doesn't want that. We could give him oxygen, but he doesn't need to be in a hospital for that. Dave, Deb, and I agree that we need to honor John's wishes. It's hard to say, but I manage to speak: "John, we will respect your choice and make the necessary arrangements to get you out of here."

It is, I now realize, the first time I've ever called him by his first name. It just tumbled out of my mouth, and I wonder if he caught it. As close as we are, it's always seemed more proper to refer to him as "Dr. Gallagher." But we've never been this intimate. He will always be my teacher, my guide, but now—at least for the moment—he's also my patient. He's John.

While he waits in the ICU for the paperwork to be completed and for transport back to his apartment, I return home and explain what's happened to Janet and Bobbi. I'm trying to stay focused by talking about the science of Gallagher's situation and probably not even making sense, but Bobbi listens intently and then says, "Why don't you get him a bed in a room that has a bathroom?"

Realizing the brilliance of this simple solution, I call Gallagher on his cellphone. To my surprise, he says, "Sure, great idea. I guess I could stay."

Since the ICU doesn't have bathrooms, we find a room

with the proper facilities on a different floor overseen by family practice doctors. They aren't accustomed to treating critically ill patients, however, and John's almost too weak to get to the toilet by himself. He's humiliated, and on top of that, he's getting sicker: The diarrhea isn't improving, he's dehydrated, and his blood oxygen levels are continuing to drop.

I'M BACK AT WORK THE NEXT DAY WHEN DEB COMES IN AND says, "Get over to Moses; Gallagher needs you. I'll take the rest of your shift."

When I get to the hospital, he's in the bathroom, and we talk through the bathroom door. "Look at what my life has come to," he says. "This isn't what I want."

He's back in bed when Kathleen arrives. She gives him Imodium while I pump fluids into him via an IV line. When it's just the three of us, there's a moment of calm— and maybe a moment of hope or lucidity, or both, for John. Maybe it's resignation—not to his fate, but to the fact that we, the people who love him, are going to fight for him every step of the way. He looks at me and says that I'm now *officially* in charge of his medical care.

He is not doing this because I'm the best doctor or because I know more about Covid-19. On both those accounts, there are plenty of physicians at Montefiore who far surpass me. Rather, he's leaving the decisions to me because I know how to get things done. And he knows I'm not afraid to ruffle feathers. My dad taught me how to stand up for what I believe in. Richard Koeppel taught me that kindness and compassion are essential to good doctoring. And Gallagher tied that all together. Right now, I'm going to need every bit of that wisdom.

At home that night, I mention that Gallagher might benefit from remdesivir, the experimental antiviral that was initially developed to treat Ebola. The Food and Drug Administration (FDA) hasn't approved remdesivir for Covid yet, so you have to apply for what is called a "compassionate use exemption" to use it on a patient. It's the same appeal Deb made for her parents, only to see it rejected. Such a request involves filling out a bunch of detailed paperwork, and Bobbi, eager for any kind of medical experience, jumps at the chance to complete the application for me.

We file the forms electronically, and within an hour I begin getting calls from hospital administration. It turns out Montefiore is participating in a clinical trial to test the drug's effectiveness on Covid, and my petition makes it appear as if I'm trying to do an end run around that. (The truth is, I knew nothing about the trial.) Gallagher's application is rejected, but I decide to try again. I call Peter Semczuk and explain to him that I want Gallagher to be put on remdesivir. I admit that I've gotten things jammed up by not being aware of the trial, but I think this medication is going to help John. I can't imagine the hoops Pete jumped through, but within twenty-four hours Gallagher is getting remdesivir.

The next day, I call the hospital's chairman of medicine, Dr. Yaron Tomer. Medical organizations are hierarchical, and this is probably as big a breach of command protocol as anyone could commit. There is a pecking order at hospitals, and ordinary docs don't call department chairs; chairs call one another. (I've seen Gallagher summarily dismiss attending physicians' requests by saying, "Have your chair call me.") But Tomer takes my call. I plead with him to allow John to get convalescent plasma, which our clinical experience has shown can be a very helpful tool in lessening Covid symptoms and promoting recovery. (It won't be officially authorized by the FDA for use in Covid until August.)

Later that day, the plasma is hanging from Gallagher's IV stand, right next to the remdesivir, and I watch his eyes widen as the plasma goes in. When the nurse moves to discard the fluid remaining in the IV tubing, Gallagher stops her to make sure he gets every last milliliter.

This moment is huge. Gallagher's participation, even in something as routine as making sure a fluid bag is completely empty, shows that he's invested, that he's taking charge of his own care. When I stop by the following day, he presents as remarkably altered, laughing one minute, crying the next. These are possible indications of Covid-related cognitive issues, but he's animated, even when he's raving, and that's a good sign.

. . .

GALLAGHER'S LUNGS ARE FILLED WITH FLUID, AND THE DOC-
tors on the family practice floor who are treating him make
the decision to do what's called "running a patient dry." It's
exactly what it sounds like: withholding fluids in the hope
that the lungs will clear and the patient will be able to
breathe easier. Normally, and in the right circumstances, it's
sound medical practice. But not when a patient is experiencing severe diarrhea and the dehydration that comes with
it. The lack of fluids is making Gallagher's condition worse,
and it's threatening the efficacy of the potentially lifesaving
treatments we've worked so hard to get him. His kidneys
are on the verge of failure. Gallagher himself is in and out
of consciousness, but in his waking moments he is lucid
enough to know that being run dry will likely kill him, and
he tells the attending physician that he doesn't approve of
the practice. Then he calls me.

I grab two liters of saline from the emergency room
downstairs, get it up to Gallagher, and squeeze the liquid
into his IV line fast. This works for the moment, but it also
makes it very clear that the family practice floor—in-room
toilets or not—isn't the right place for Gallagher. He's drifting in and out of consciousness, and since he's put me in
charge, I make a decision that I'm sure he's not going to
like: I send him back to the ICU.

He's now been in the hospital for four nights. Kathleen
stays with him that night and for the next several, sleeping
in a chair next to his bed. She's been part of a group practice at Jacobi Medical Center for more than thirty years, but

now she decides to take a month off from her primary care work. She monitors John's treatment, the two IVs, and the phlebitis (inflammation of the veins) in his arms.

When he wakes up on the fifth day, he has no idea where he is. He still feels the humiliation, but now the physical pain is gone. Later, he'll tell us that he remembers thinking before he was admitted to the hospital, *Boy, the odds are bad.* And as he started to feel sicker and sicker, he thought, *I'm probably going to buy it from this, but there are worse ways to die, lots of worse ways.*

Gallagher is fighting, but we still aren't sure that the battle can be won. As many as 20 percent of the patients admitted to ICUs die, according to a 2014 study. If there's hopeful news in that statistic, it's that 85 percent of those who die are on a ventilator. Gallagher, at the moment, is the only patient in the ICU who isn't intubated. Instead, we are turning him and giving him high-flow nasal oxygen.

I think that he needs rest as much as anything else, but that's almost impossible due to the incessant beeping. The monitors in an ICU far outnumber those in an ordinary hospital room, and they all chirp and buzz. There's also a speaker right next to Gallagher's ear, and it's constantly crackling to life with voices and sounds from across the unit. I make a call, and over comes Fernando, one of the maintenance guys I've helped several times with medical issues. He isn't allowed into the room, but he hands me a miniature screwdriver and talks me through disconnecting the speaker.

The next day, Gallagher thanks me for a good night's sleep and, somehow recalling that Fernando was there, says, "Another of your private patients?"

I keep the pocket-sized tool, making a mental note to reconnect the speaker once this has all played out.

Given Covid's twists and often rapid downturns, Gallagher is by no means out of the woods. In fact, the next day his breathing becomes more labored, and his body appears to be shutting down. The ICU attending calls Dave and me to come in. "You need to pay your last respects," she says. I call Deb, Angelo, and Dr. Mike Jones, another of Gallagher's protégés. Dave calls a few more people. We all go into his room, one by one.

PART III

May–September 2020

By the end of May, 100,000 new Covid infections are being recorded daily, and Dr. Anthony Fauci, director of the National Institute of Allergy and Infectious Diseases, tells Congress that these numbers are likely understated. At the same time, physicians on every continent are learning new methods for handling the virus, and new treatments are being developed, making Covid more survivable.

New York is beginning to see fewer cases. May 29 marks the first day since the pandemic began that Montefiore does not record a Covid-19 death. The consensus is that areas hit hard early by the pandemic have learned to manage future outbreaks through wearing masks, washing hands, and adopting social distancing and isolation policies. Now the bulk of the fatalities are occurring in places like Florida, Wisconsin, and Texas, states where isolation measures have been only reluctantly pursued, if at all.

Treatment is also shifting. The antimalarial hydroxychloroquine, which showed early promise against the virus, is by early June mostly discredited, as the British medical journal *The Lancet* and *The New England Journal of Medicine* retract studies that appeared to indicate the medication was effective. Other treatments, including two being studied at Montefiore—convalescent plasma and remdesivir—prove to be more successful, and their use contributes to a drop in fatalities, if not infections.

One problem that's becoming increasingly clear is the disproportionate effect Covid-19 has on minority communities. A paper published on June 24 in the journal *EClinicalMedicine* (thirteen of whose fourteen co-authors are Montefiore physicians) states: "Black individuals have been disproportionately affected. U.S. counties that are majority-Black have three times the rate of infection and almost six times the rate of death as counties where White residents are in the majority." This disparity is especially stark in New York City, the paper continues, where "boroughs with the highest proportion of Black and Hispanic residents reported the worst outcomes."

Other studies confirm that one of Covid's ripple effects has been to increase mortality rates among people who didn't have the virus, possibly because they were too afraid to seek medical care when they experienced symptoms that would otherwise have led them to consult a physician.

Dozens of journals report this phenomenon, and two research projects at Montefiore reveal that out-of-hospital cardiac arrest cases and deaths have increased by more than 300 percent during the pandemic. Another study has found that patients undergoing treatment at Montefiore's cancer clinics are more likely to die of Covid than those without underlying disease. This is just the beginning of what will likely be a years-long examination of the virus's deadly and devastating corollary effects.

More and more, families are struggling not just with the disease but also with the effects of attempts to contain the disease. According to UNESCO, about 90 percent of the world's school-attending children—about 1.5 billion kids—are facing shuttered classrooms. As the school year comes to an end in America, parents wonder how they'll manage over the summer. Across the United States, more than 70 percent of the summer camps and local daytime recreation programs have announced that they won't be operating at all or will be operating with vastly limited attendance and hours.

Applications for unemployment benefits are also skyrocketing. Although the number of people filing new claims has peaked, more than 1 million people are still making their initial filings every week, and by June 20, 33 million Americans are jobless—a number that dwarfs the high reached during the Great Depression by 500 percent.

By the end of June, multiple vaccine trials are under way, but questions remain about whether the vaccines will be effective, how they'll be distributed, and how much they'll cost. On June 30, the European Union reopens its borders, but citing the increasing number of cases in America, it specifically excludes travelers from the United States.

The regional distribution of Covid continues to shift in July. *The New York Times* reports record numbers of new cases seven times during the first eleven days of the month. But New York City is doing much better, and at Montefiore the number of daily initial infections descends into the single digits, where it will stay until late fall. Stockpiles of protective equipment have been replenished, and fatalities— thanks to better drugs and hard-won experience—are down.

The geographic migration of Covid continues in the United States in August. Mississippi becomes the state with the highest positivity rate, while in New York, where cases are declining, Governor Andrew Cuomo announces that schools will reopen in the fall if current trends continue. In September, the school year begins with a patchwork of policies and restrictions. On September 6, the United States surpasses six million cases. More and more, the biggest fear is that the disease will roar back as students return to classrooms and as the cold weather sets in and more people gather indoors. Those predictions begin to come true as the country hits seven million cases on September 25.

By October, Covid—or, more accurately, how people view Covid—has become the primary issue in the upcoming presidential election. This fact is brought home on October 2, when President Donald J. Trump and First Lady

Melania Trump test positive for the virus. By the third week of the month, there's little doubt that a "second wave" is in full swing. Cases in New York are rising, leading to spot closures of schools and businesses. On October 20, the United States reports 58,387 new infections—a number not seen since July. As Halloween approaches, communities struggle with how to manage trick-or-treating and whether to cancel it altogether. Some households rig up chutes made out of PVC tubing to deliver candy to trick-or-treaters.

By November 3, Election Day in the United States, nearly 10 million Americans have been infected with the virus. The number of deaths is approaching 250,000. Worldwide, there are 45 million confirmed cases, and 1.25 million people have died.

Chapter Twelve

When I walk into Gallagher's room to pay my last respects, I freeze. I don't know what to say, and I feel like a disappointment to him, as both a doctor and a friend. I want to apologize for failing him, but I also want to tell him what he's meant to me. I want to tell him that every single patient I've ever helped, every life I've ever saved, is a result of what he taught me. I want to thank him for the life—my family, my home, the way I think and see the world—that he gave me.

What I really want to do is tell him that I love him.

But instead, I fight back tears. Instead, I fail to say good-bye. Because I can't accept this outcome.

I step out of the room and begin to cry. Dave Esses puts his arm around me, and another doctor, Caron Campbell,

embraces me as well. They tell me that I didn't fail Gallagher, and that they've always seen my friendship with him
as something special, something they wish they had. We're
all going to be lost without our mentor.

WE'VE DONE ALL WE CAN. MEDICALLY, THOSE TERRIBLE
words, full of hidden meaning, hang in the air. There is no
practical hope left. The kind of hope that remains isn't
grounded in science, in logic, in sound medical practice. It's
grounded in something more mysterious. There are patients who die when you think they're going to live, and
there are patients who live when you have every expecta-
tion that they will die. I call this a matter of statistics repre-
senting either end of the bell curve. Others might call it
something else.

Before Gallagher got sick, he and I had a conversation
about faith. Knowing that he'd rebelled against his Catholic
upbringing by embracing science, I read him an amusing
document that Richard Koeppel had given me. He wrote it
when he was old enough to worry about death, to make his
wishes clear. The document is called "Morbid Thoughts,"
and this is what it says: "I write this because my mind is on
death. You can do what you want with my body and have
any kind of service. I only have three requests, which are:
No rabbi at any service; they are whores. No mention of
God at any service; God does not exist. No prayers." You

should have seen the look on John's face. He broke into a huge grin and then pumped his fist. "Right on," he said.

Nevertheless, Deb White enters John's room hiding something in her hand: a bottle of sacred oil. Her mother got it from St. Anthony's, the family parish, and gave it to Deb a decade earlier. Deb has used the contents sparingly. She'd hoped to apply it to her father when he was ill, but she never got the chance. She is determined not to miss this opportunity. She anoints Gallagher, an avowed and committed atheist, with the oil. Deb, who has seen more and lost more than any doctor in the hospital, is reverting to the most basic and ancient traditions of our work, attempting, when all hope is lost, to bring the heavens into play. Silently, she prays. I hope she's able to muster the words that I couldn't—to tell him she loves him.

When she comes out of the room, she declares with total confidence that Gallagher is not going to die. In spite of all the science, in spite of his having the worst chest X-ray I've ever seen, in spite of all the patients in exactly the same state whom we've seen die, Deb's faith gives me something to hold on to. I don't know whether I believe in God, but I sure as hell believe in Deb White.

GALLAGHER SPENDS ANOTHER TWO WEEKS IN THE ICU. HE has ups and downs. There's a moment when he insists that I discharge him, but we manage to keep him in the ICU. I spend twenty-one consecutive days caring for him, and he steadily shows some improvement. Eventually, Kathleen begins arranging for something we didn't dare think about before: what happens next.

It's likely that he will spend weeks, maybe even more, in rehab. His lung capacity is shot. His muscles have atrophied. He remembers almost nothing since well before that first night I went to his apartment. But he knows that I've tried to help him. He knows that getting him this far has taken a huge effort.

HEALING COMES SLOWLY WITH MANY COVID PATIENTS, BUT there's a point where those who have been sick seem to know that they're going to make it. For Gallagher, that happens one morning into his second week in the ICU, when a nurse enters the room with a cheerful greeting. Noticing that his condition has improved, she says, "Dr. Gallagher, you're looking much better, even healthy." Gallagher grumbles that he could still die, but I don't think he believes it. When the nurse leaves, he says that he hates it when people tell him how good he looks. So before I go, I make sure to remark that he looks and sounds like crap.

It might seem obvious, but with Covid, as with so much in medicine, it all comes down to time and care. Even with a virus this lethal, our weapons are still the basic ones: oxygen, IV fluids, Imodium. If we can help patients breathe, keep them hydrated, slow down the digestive tract, then we can tilt the scale ever so slightly—but significantly—toward survival.

When he is well enough, Gallagher is transferred to Montefiore's Burke Rehabilitation Hospital, just over the Westchester County border. It's a calm facility surrounded by trees and wide lawns. Gallagher hates it. His mind is too restless. He doesn't like being confined to a wheelchair and dragging an oxygen tank around while wearing an embarrassing hospital gown.

He confides that being a patient is every bit as bad as he thought it would be. After fifty years in emergency medicine, half of those spent as chair of the emergency department at Montefiore, his experience as a hospital patient confirms that the healthcare system is still in need of reform. He says it's all about making things easy and cushy for the doctors and nurses and for squeezing every ounce of revenue out of every possible opportunity.

I tell him I'm glad to see he's getting his energy back.

He's also been observing the doctor who's caring for his roommate, a retired New York City sanitation department worker with a pension. The patient is a little shaky and disoriented. He was living alone but managing until he slipped and fell, bashed his head and got a traumatic brain bleed, and ended up in rehab. His doctor comes in maybe once every other day and says only one thing to this poor guy: "Do you have any questions for me?"

The fellow doesn't have a clue what the doctor is asking or what *he* should be asking in return. He knows he's in a hospital of some kind, but he's not really clear where. He can sometimes get close on the number of days he's spent in the hospital, but his count is never exact. His condition is improving, but he's filled with doubt and fear. Gallagher, weak as he is, is outraged by the poor quality of care.

"It's everywhere," Gallagher confides, his voice still raspy from coughing so much. "This is just the most immediate example right in front of me, the most flagrant. I look at this doctor, and I have contempt for him. He doesn't know when I'm looking at him that I'm thinking, *If you were working in my department, we'd be in the office right now talking about how you're supposed to treat people like they're your mom.*"

GALLAGHER CREDITS ME WITH SAVING HIS LIFE. BUT IT WAS our team, it was time and oxygen and persistence, and especially, from a medical standpoint, it was his do not intubate directive. Because a ventilator was unequivocally ruled out, we had to come up with other strategies. That's a lesson. Maybe Dave, Kathleen, and I were the only ones who could have gotten Gallagher out of his apartment and into the hospital, or maybe somebody else could have done the same. What's important is that one of the most important doctors in the history of emergency medicine—a person whose vision and philosophy now extend into just about every emergency room in America and beyond—walks out of rehab on his own.

Gallagher says he learned about respecting human dignity from his mother and that you either get this quality of empathy and caring from a parent or you don't. Four years after my mother died, he told me he thought I'd received it from my parents. By all accounts, my mother was a supremely empathic person. Hearing him say that meant something to me. It helped me understand what I was doing in medicine, why helping people was so important.

A few weeks after being discharged from rehab, Gallagher officially retires. And he does something he's never done before: He invites me to visit him at his lake house. Gallagher's desire for privacy has always meant that his homes are his special, private places. Especially this cabin— kind of like Rockaway Beach is for me, but without another soul around.

One day, we swim out to the middle of the lake together. And when we're there, staying perfectly still, barely making a ripple in the water's surface, he says, "I'm here because of you."

Gallagher thrives on making me uncomfortable, and he knows that nothing makes me more so than this kind of raw expression of emotion. So I take a deep breath and disappear beneath the surface. Of course, it feels good to have my efforts acknowledged, but it isn't necessary to thank me. He saved my life, too. I love being a doctor, and he, more than anyone else, has made me a better one.

Chapter Thirteen

There was a moment during the spring when hearses made slow processions through New York City neighborhoods. Each vehicle contained the body of a loved one. The drivers were given the addresses of the deceased's survivors, the next of kin, and those bereaved families and friends leaned out their windows, sat on their stoops, and stood still on the sidewalks, giving the only (inadequate) goodbye they were allowed. The refrigerated trucks, each of which held ninety or more bodies, sometimes allowed all-too-brief "identification ceremonies," where a single family member could observe for a moment, from a safe distance, the loved one's body being taken out of the truck for transport to the crematorium in order to make sure it was the right person.

We all understand that funerals can provide closure, a chance to remember, a chance to perform the final rites of passage, to transfer responsibility and affection and hope from those who have departed to those who survive. Saying goodbye to loved ones in a formal setting is a practice as old as humanity itself. I keep thinking about how funerals stopped once Covid started. Deb's father didn't get a fully proper one. Neither did most of the souls Sean so carefully transported to the refrigerated trucks. Instead, in some cases we resorted to mass graves. Think about that: mass graves in twenty-first-century America. On Hart Island, where before Covid prisoners used to bury about a dozen bodies each week, more workers were needed as the number of interments went up by a factor of five or more. Fifty, eighty, even a hundred people were buried every few days, anonymous and alone.

But now, in midsummer, there are reasons to be hopeful. More patients afflicted with the virus are surviving and recovering, including John Gallagher, Deb's mom, and countless others. We know that isolation works: My eighty-five-year-old father and tens of thousands of others are alive because of it. I'm happy that two of the most important people in my life are still with me. But I keep remembering the last funeral I attended. My friend Tom, who also works at the hospital, lost his father in February. His dad was ninety-five and had metastatic kidney cancer that went into his bones. He fought hard for his life and never complained.

He was stoic and thankful for the time he had on this earth, and he made the most of every day. Everyone at the hospital loves Tom, so the church was filled with his co-workers.

I was overwhelmed with an unusual anxiety. Covid was just beginning, though it was still seen mostly as an overseas problem. Scanning the room filled with elderly people and close friends that day, I was suddenly gripped with panic at the thought that I might be carrying some disease, that I might infect everyone. So I moved to a seat in the back. It was hard to sit still.

My co-workers who were at the funeral sensed my apprehension. My other colleagues at work sensed it. My family sensed it. But it was a vague sensation, almost a premonition. It wasn't enough, or at least it didn't seem like it was enough, to act on. I didn't know exactly what I was so afraid of, until everything started happening—the infections, the deaths, the prohibited memorials. How could any of us have known that in a matter of weeks, those essential rituals that bring us all together in our grief would become forbidden, something nearly impossible to engage in?

I've always believed that no matter what, you never stop, you always keep moving. It isn't necessarily the most thoughtful or reflective way to live, and maybe I am this way because of fear: fear of standing still, of not progressing, of stagnating. But it's also a suitable attitude for an emergency room doctor. Remember, we're all about the first sixty minutes of any illness or accident. We take care of what needs to be taken care of and move on. When my mother was killed by a drunk driver, I was just months into my first semester of medical school and was offered a leave of absence. I didn't take it. I just worked that much harder. I've never been afraid of failure, but I've always been terrified of quitting. Hanging over the desk where I studied at night as a child was a poster with a quote from an 1883 speech on the duties of American citizenship by Theodore Roosevelt:

> It is not the critic who counts; not the man who points out how the strong man stumbles, or where the doer of deeds could have done them better. The credit belongs to the man who is actually in the arena, whose face is marred by dust and sweat and blood; who strives valiantly; who errs, who comes short again and again, because there is no effort without error and shortcoming.

My dad hung the poster there for me. I returned the favor for my daughter. And I still think about that quote. Not the "no effort without error" part. I think about "the man who is actually in the arena." And every day, I make a decision to stay in.

Until this year, fear was not part of my conscious vocabulary. In some ways, the most obvious manifestation of my newfound apprehension is how I've stopped talking about what is going on at work with my wife, my kids, and my friends. I don't like thinking that the people who love me and count on me might see fear in me. But I know that I've been colder than I want to be, that I appear to care less than I do.

In May, as the number of Covid cases we were seeing began to decrease, we didn't let our guard down. But as Memorial Day approached, everybody in the ER, everybody in our hospital, maybe everyone in our city, breathed a sigh of relief. The numbers went from thousands of Covid patients, to hundreds, to dozens, to just a few. Maybe the onslaught was coming to an end.

But the streets were still mostly abandoned. Restaurants and bars remained closed. Schools never reopened. The playgrounds were empty, the old-fashioned sprinklers attached to fire hydrants—the ones that have always kept Bronx kids cool during the summer months—stood dry and untapped. What really made me realize that the world had changed and that things might never return to normal was the cancellation of the camping season at Southwoods, the camp owned by my friend Scott Ralls.

Scott had been battling metastatic cancer of the tonsils, but the previous summer he'd insisted that camp must go on and that he had to be there, even when he lost his ability to eat. One night, he drove down to Montefiore, and I arranged to have a feeding tube surgically placed in his abdomen. The kids at Southwoods never knew how sick he was.

Scott would find a private place, unbutton his shirt, and pour the nutritional liquid into his belly. He never missed a boat race or a singalong or a kickball game.

Scott would have been a great ER doctor. His ability to multitask was unparalleled. He took his responsibility for the five hundred campers entrusted to his care very seriously. He paid attention to every detail and was incapable of delegating. He really got to know his campers, taking in every detail about their lives.

Scott also taught me how to manage people without them realizing they were being managed, an invaluable skill in the daily functioning of an emergency room. Having a nurse, a physician's assistant, and an X-ray technician all working *with* you, as opposed to *for* you, makes all the difference with respect to patient care.

Scott trusted me with his health. Sometimes too much, like when he had a heart attack, and he called me instead of calling an ambulance. But I was complicit in this arrangement because I lied to him. When he was still lucid, after his second stroke, he asked me, "Doc, is this the beginning of the end?" I knew that his disease had spread, not only to his brain and lungs but also to his bones, intestines, and liver. But I told him to hang in there and that I believed there was a concoction out there for him that would work. He just had to be patient.

Did I say this because I can never give up? Because I myself cannot accept death? Was I responding to his need for me to say there was hope for him? Or was I quite simply not man enough to tell him the truth? That decision will haunt me for the rest of my life. I was his doctor and trusted friend, but I didn't have the courage and decency to be honest with him.

Scott was devastated when camp was canceled because of Covid. He thought about all those kids, about how they needed one another, needed him, and needed the summer break. And after months of lockdown, he knew the parents needed the break from their kids as well. Scott wanted more than anything to be there for them.

He didn't want special treatment. He knew that in the midst of this pandemic, the shadow of death was on everybody, that it was sweeping the world. Scott suffered with his illness, but he wasn't the type to put his pain above others'. He was brave. He stayed in the arena. And I did what I could to buy him time, cheer him on, and ease his suffering.

In his final days, Scott did what he did best: He gave me something. By entrusting his care to me, by allowing me to hope, by accepting the hope I offered him, Scott made me feel like a helper again. He gave me back something that Covid had taken away.

I was sitting at Scott's bedside and he motioned me close. When I leaned in, he said, "Fourteen-seven-five?"

Then he said, "Three-one-zero?"

This didn't make any sense to me. But then suddenly, I understood: He was asking me how much time he had left. The question turned into a plea when I looked into his eyes. He'd fought so hard to live, to have more time with his wife, Andrea, and their kids. But he'd been worn down by pain. Was he asking me to help him die? I believe I would have helped him if Andrea had suggested the need to hasten his death or if Scott had signaled his desire to me. But the moment passed, and Scott didn't ask. He was dying, but he clung to life.

It was heart-wrenching watching my good friend slip away, but I didn't cry. I found myself thinking about the patients who had died in the ER without their loved ones at their side. I couldn't get it out of my head: all those lost goodbyes. And here was Scott, facing death in the way all of those other people should have had the chance to face it. His passing was so unfair, but it stood against a backdrop of so many deaths that felt equally, if not more, unjust.

How far we'd come this year, I thought, to appreciate the privilege of having a peaceful death surrounded by love. A death like Deb's dad had, with Deb at his side, or like John Gallagher would have had if he hadn't survived. How rare that basic human experience of having a loved one present at one's death had become. How tragic that we've learned that such a death isn't guaranteed, no matter how advanced our society, no matter what medicine can do.

IT'S EARLY SEPTEMBER, AND I'M ON A SHIFT WHEN I RECEIVE a text from Andrea. She describes Scott's breathing, which sounds like that of a dying person to me. I tell her what to do, and she does it, without asking whether or not it will hasten his death. I advise doubling his fentanyl and scopolamine patches and his morphine elixir to ensure his comfort. He hasn't had water in days, and I worry that hypernatremia (a high concentration of sodium in the blood) will cause a seizure. If so, will Andrea panic and call 911? Will Scott have to face death in a hospital? But it doesn't happen. Scott stops breathing and dies at 3:00 P.M. I leave work, pick up Janet, and get to Scott and Andrea's just after 4:00 as the hospice nurse is cleaning him up.

Scott's mouth hanging open is disconcerting to Andrea. It would be too much for their ninth-grade daughter, Bailey, to see. So I grab some gauze and wrap it around his head, the way I did for the father of the young woman grieving his death in the Covid Zone, the way Angelo Recine did for his mother when she died.

After Bailey says goodbye to her father, as I help the hospice nurse with further cleaning of the body, I accidentally drop Scott's leg. Andrea, who believes Scott is looking down on us, gives me a hard time about it.

I sign the death certificate. And once again, it's personal. This is my friend's end-of-life document. I'm not filling out the paperwork for a list of unfamiliar names. But as I sign for Scott, I feel like I'm signing for every person I've watched die in the ER. I wish that I could have given them more. I want to believe that every person who dies under our care is mourned properly, but I know that's not the case. The refrigerated trucks, the orange bags, the gurneys crowded against one another, the praying, the dying—those are my memories of Covid, and they are real. And they are important. We may not be able to stop the next pandemic, but we can be better prepared if we don't forget this one.

Chapter Fourteen

When the pandemic started, the one person I feared I was most at risk of losing was the person in my life who has lost the most. My dad turned eighty-five in January 2020, and he's strong as hell. Before the lockdown, he worked out three days a week, going to the gym to lift weights and walk the treadmill. But that wouldn't keep him from being vulnerable to Covid. He protested loudly about it, but I laid down the law. I told him that he had to self-quarantine, that he could no longer leave the house, and that I would take care of whatever he needed.

So twice a week, usually once on a weekend and once after a shift, I'd drive down to the Rockaways and leave him groceries and household supplies. We'd see each other through the window, but I was so terrified of getting him sick that I didn't dare go inside. Still, he'd let me know how he felt by calling me while I was driving home, usually to give me grief about a bruised apple or paying fifty cents too much for a bunch of broccoli. We kept up this routine as the pandemic raged on, as hospitals across New York City swelled with the ranks of the elderly, like my dad, but who weren't fortunate enough to have somebody to care for them, let alone have that person be a doctor.

I allowed my dad one exception to his quarantine, and that was a trip to the mailbox. Dad's lifeline to the world is sending letters. There are a few people at the hospital, including John Gallagher, with whom he corresponds regularly, sending them everything from newspaper clippings to crossword puzzles.

He calls folks at the hospital, too. I know it isn't typical for your parent to make friends with your co-workers, but that's my dad: He's interested in everyone, and he finds a way to connect. And the funny thing is, although I sometimes get tired of spending so much time on the phone with him, other folks don't mind. I'll be walking down the hall, and somebody will tell me, with a big grin on their face, that they "got a call from Duke," my dad's nickname. During the Covid pandemic, though, Dad stopped talking to his friends who work at the hospital. Isolation seems to beget isolation, and I assume he withdrew because he just couldn't bear the idea of knowing that any of them might come to harm.

For my dad, grief is not just indivisible. It is universal and ubiquitous. My mom died when she was forty-six years old, eight years younger than I am now. For a long time, I used to think that if she came back to life, she could just slip back into their house, because everything was still the way she left it. Today, more than thirty years later, it still looks just as it did when they went to dinner that night: her things still tucked neatly into her drawers, her dresses hanging in the closet, her shoes paired on racks next to his. Her makeup, her jewelry, it's all there. Sometimes I think, *Is that love?*

I was twenty years old when my mother was killed. It was hard to get through my medical training and be there for my dad, but he tried not to burden me with his sorrow. We both ended up talking a lot to my father's cousin Richard Koeppel about it. He was a good listener, and because of that my dad and I didn't collapse into each other's grief. We supported each other, but both of us knew that we couldn't console each other, because our loss was the same.

With my mom gone, I knew my dad needed my attention, and maybe it was being able to give that to him that kept me from going off the deep end. Three years later, my sister died of cancer. It's impossible to say which death hurt him more. Anyone could tell you that my dad didn't know how he'd survive without my mom, though he did survive, as best he could. But my sister's death shook him to the core.

In the neighborhood where Janet and I live now, if somebody dies, people cook for the family every day for as long as months. But that stopped when the Covid pandemic began. For a while, you couldn't even order a take-out meal to help ease the burden of a bereaved family. All these little things that vanished add up to a deep sense of isolation. There's so much more to it than just being locked in a house. Sometimes, working in a place that's so crowded and busy, I forget that even with tragedy all around me, the real heartbreak is experienced by people who have nobody.

AFTER ONE OF MY EARLY SUMMER SHIFTS, I DIAL MY DAD from my car. It's 7:11 P.M. I usually call right at 7:00, so he says, "I was about to phone you." I want to say, *I'm not that late,* but I can picture him sitting at the kitchen table, waiting for his old-fashioned landline to ring. Dad never asks what's going on in the emergency room, and I don't tell him. Why give him things to worry about? But sometimes keeping my experiences to myself leaves me feeling disconnected from him.

I think of all the things I cannot say to him: *Covid travels through the air. I don't have the proper protection. I can't sleep. I'm worried I'll infect Janet and the kids. My good friend Scott is facing his last days. John Gallagher is ill. There's no cure for Covid, and nobody knows when or if there will be. When I'm at work, every minute feels like a day. I'm scared.*

Instead, I say, "But I beat you to it, didn't I?"

I let him tell me about his day. His severely arthritic

knee has been giving him trouble. He has a walker, but he won't use it. When I asked Gallagher for advice about how to get my dad to use the device, he said, "You don't."

I said, "I don't what?"

Typical Gallagher, he said, "He's gonna fall and crack his head open, and he's on a blood thinner, so he's gonna die. You have to honor that. You want him to use the walker for you, but he doesn't want to be seen as an old man."

Gallagher was only half serious. I'm going to keep nagging my dad about the walker, but right now I tell him that he could get a steroid injection to ease his discomfort. Dad says he'll do it, so I tell him I'll drive down the next day and take him to a local orthopedist for the shot.

I think, *I need a break*. We take a family vacation every year, usually to someplace exotic—Peru, Tanzania, Vietnam. Over the past few months, I've found myself fantasizing about getting away. Somewhere far off and quiet. But there's no travel happening, and that's led my thoughts to a different place: to the idea of retirement. Maybe I'll do what Richard Koeppel did. When he got to be in his mid-fifties, he wanted to travel, but he also still wanted to see patients, to feel the excitement that so many ER docs crave. So he found that small hospital, the one with a caseload that fluctuated by the season. Most of the year, things were quiet, and Richard had plenty of time for his hobbies, for travel, for friends. In the summer, when vacationers filled the resort town, his ER would get as busy and intense as many city emergency rooms. Is that the kind of perfect balance I want? I want the death and the sadness to stop, but I'm not going to make it stop by running away from it. I'm not saying a cushy retirement isn't in my future, but this pandemic is happening on my watch, on Deb's watch, on Angelo's. We're going to ride it out. We're not going anywhere.

THE DUTY OF A DOCTOR IS TO TREAT THE SICK AND, IF YOU GO back to Hippocrates, to protect your patients from harm and injustice. If you do this, you don't have to worry about what you feel as a person because it's not all that important. But like all great ideas, things change when you put them into practice. Covid came as the greatest challenge to the Hippocratic oath. What if your patient's head is slumped over on her shoulder? What if she's gasping for air? What if she looks just like the guy next to her and the woman next to him? None of them can talk to you about advance directives, their families aren't allowed in the emergency room, and they are only three people in a long line of others who need your help if they are to survive. What should you do to save them? Or what if your beloved mentor states that his wish is to die?

My friend Tom asked me what would be the hardest thing to carry with me after this is over. I live by the creed "Do no harm." But Covid-19 has done harm, not by a lack of medical competence or goodwill, but because it is a disease that doctors—and an entire medical profession, an entire nation, an entire world—was not prepared to handle. Everything we have done and not done to treat Covid—giving hydroxychloroquine, steroids, anticoagulants; intubation; proning—every success and every failure, has come as part of an ever-evolving process. The learning curve has been steep in a way I've never seen before during my years as a physician and hope to never see again. Never in my career have I seen doctors turning to one another and saying, "How are we going to do it today?" In Deb's words, "It wasn't just that we didn't have what we needed. It's that we didn't know what we didn't know." Everybody expects modern medicine, with all this technology and data at its command, to be able to handle a challenge like this. But the truth is that medicine, government, and the whole world has failed.

All over the country, in the onslaught of the Covid spring, when people came to ERs gasping for breath, they were put on ventilators. It was the medically correct thing to do. Then, over a period of weeks, doctors began to see that there was an alternative. The information about proning spread almost as quickly as the virus itself, and with it we were able to do something different.

I remember in the beginning, before the Blue Zone became the Covid Zone, a fifty-five-year-old guy was brought in. He was disheveled, unkempt, likely homeless. He had a cough but no fever. He told us he had night sweats and weight loss, and he proceeded to cough up blood. It was TB, no doubt. We took him to one of our six isolation rooms. He got up to pee, slipped, fell down, and cried out. The first person through the door to reach him didn't hesitate to help him, without regard for PPE, though there was blood all over the floor. They just went in, and their intervention calmed him down, gave him the comfort he needed. That would be a much more difficult call now. It wouldn't make sense to rush in unprotected. But if a patient was in that kind of dire need and nobody was gowned up, I want to believe each and every one of us would go in anyway.

Covid has rewritten the rules. We remain compassionate caregivers, but we do so knowing that the system failed us. We couldn't predict the cascade of challenges wrought by a global pandemic. Maybe there should have been better planning. But in the end, I know what matters most is that we've shown up. We've practiced the best medicine we can, with the tools we have, not the tools we wish were available. It's almost too trite to say we'll do better next time, but we will. We have to. And most people who know—the world's best epidemiologists—say that there *will* be a next time. Maybe one day we'll look back at Covid as a learning experience that helped us in the following decades, just as the medical profession has looked back at the flu pandemic of 1918–19 to better understand Covid today.

IT'S TRUE THAT AT A CERTAIN POINT I BECAME DETACHED. It was after Mark Fenig and I took that walk in the East Village to the applause of people in their buildings. That felt good, but I feel embarrassed about it now. I think about the refrigerated trucks and hearses snaking through similar neighborhoods, and the silent, stricken tributes that were offered along that journey. I feel embarrassed when anyone calls me a hero. Not with all those bodies. I'm not a hero. I'm a doctor. A scared doctor—scared, just like everyone else.

We're not talking about five, six, seven deaths in a day. Back in the spring and early summer, sometimes there were double or triple that. A nurse would say, "This patient's dead," and we'd walk away, move on to the next one. Was I really that cold, that callous? My wife, my colleagues, my friends, say probably not. Maybe I was protecting myself emotionally. Saving up my energy for the living. Or maybe Covid has turned me into somebody I don't like. I never thought I'd have to struggle to find my sense of compassion, but it takes a lot, when you're surrounded by misery, not to be hardened by it. Because that hardening gives you a layer of protection. The protection is effective, for sure, but the catch is that it makes you a worse doctor.

I don't like beating up on myself, but I know I'm not alone. Every doctor in the world who has fought for patients with Covid and lost feels the same way. I guarantee it. Doctors are well intentioned. But good intentions aren't always enough, and during Covid when we didn't know what we were dealing with, we couldn't help everyone.

That's something I'll have to live with. I hope I'll learn from it. Be better because of it.

And then there is justice—something I'm betting every doctor picked by John Gallagher to work in the emergency room feels strongly about. The emergency room envisioned by my mentor is a place where everybody is equal, where every life has the same value and every person receives the same care. I think our emergency room has remained that way all through Covid, but the pandemic has re-exposed a bigger problem: the inequality of healthcare in the United States in general. One of the reasons we had so many deaths at Montefiore is because life in the Bronx is hard and re-sources are scarce. All those comorbidities that have led to all those Covid fatalities in poor communities around the world were preventable in a way that Covid itself wasn't. If we'd taken better care of our communities—not just in the Bronx, but also in places like Boston and Philadelphia, which spiked early; and places like rural Wisconsin and Florida, which spiked late—as a *nation,* we'd have seen fewer deaths. But we didn't. And the Bronx, and those other communities, and America have paid for it.

BOBBI WOULD TELL YOU THAT SHE HAS BEEN INTERESTED IN medicine since she learned to speak. Specifically, emergency medicine. When she was younger and was asked why she wanted to be a doctor, she always said that it was because she wanted to be like me. To me, that's the most beautiful thing a kid can say about their parent. I'm so proud.

And now, as summer ends, Bobbi is about to fulfill that ambition. She's starting medical school. But it is medical school during the Covid era. We're receiving email after email, caution after caution. How can a medical school operate from a distance, with students isolated from one another, from clinical study, from labs and classrooms? I don't know, and Bobbi seems a little distant in the days leading up to her departure. So I suggest that we drive out to the Rockaways for one last swim in the Atlantic. Here we are, level with the horizon, the sky big and clear, with the line of water stretching out into the distance. We're jumping waves, I'm having a great time, but when I look over, she's crying. "Why are you crying?" I ask her. To make it a little easier on her, I add, "You get to say it in one word."

"Scared," she says, the tears continuing to flow.

"There's nothing I can say to get you over that feeling," I reply. But I know it will pass once she gets her first tests behind her.

Constitutionally, she's like me, all about hard work and perseverance and, yes, doubt. How does it feel to not yet have lost your innocence but to know that it will happen soon? Bobbi has studied, sacrificed, and excelled academically, all the while clinging to the safety of her childhood, knowing she's been lucky to be able to do that. But now there's medical school. There's the lease she signed and the issues of privilege that she'll face. There's the competition that drives all good doctors. Maybe—I hope—none of this is as daunting to her as it seems to me, having been through it.

When we drop her off at school, I take a deep breath. I've done this before. Four years ago, when I took her to college, I wept like a baby knowing that going forward, "home" for Bobbi would no longer be my home, that staying with me would be, for her, a visit. Now, knowing that in four years she'll be a doctor, I think, *Who will be her first death? Whose hand will she hold? Whom will she place too many fentanyl patches on in a humane effort to ease their suffering?*

Bobbi calls me every day, and at the end of the first week of classes, she sends me the "oath to medicine" that the first-year medical students have been asked to write. Hers ends this way: "Our class is a team and we all share similar goals, morals, and values. We will work together to achieve our common goal of becoming a physician. I will remember that healing is an art that requires love and that being a physician is a privilege. I will always intend to do good and I will never use my medical knowledge to do harm."

"Always." "Never." These words come so easily when you're young.

With Bobbi safely tucked away in Albany, Janet and I drive Matt to Boston. He'll live in an off-campus apartment with three friends, all of them members of a fraternity, which means that he is at high risk for exposure to Covid. During the three-hour drive, I tell myself that it is not a matter of *if* but *when* Matt will call to tell me he has a fever. When I share this thought with him, he simply says, "I'll power through." A health science major at Boston University, he doesn't worry about how this pandemic will impact his future. I envy him his feeling of invincibility, and I'll make sure he has vitamins C and D3, zinc, and turmeric, which I've instructed him to take daily (but I'll settle for once a week).

The next day, I resume teaching at the Albert Einstein College of Medicine with a brand-new class. The eight first-year medical students assigned to me are my kids, each and every one of them like my daughter, Bobbi. It blows my mind how much has changed in the past year. But in twenty-five years of teaching first-year students how to do a medical history and physical examination, I haven't changed my methods at all. I teach what I learned from Gallagher: *Listen to your patients.* This means: *Don't take notes while a patient is talking to you. Don't ask them a list of questions you've memorized.*

Why?

Because you might miss what they're trying to tell you. It's less a duty than a privilege to be able to help another human being. Respect your patients.

Just today, I received a text from a former medical school student who is now an attending physician supervising one of my students from last year. What he said was simple: *Rob, thanks for keeping it real and practical.*

Some years, it's hard to rally myself to work with a new group of students. But not this year. I see my daughter in each and every face. I hope my daughter gets from her teachers what I try to give my students.

Maybe in the future, she'll practice with me at Montefiore. If what I've read is true, that more pandemics are coming, then I hope my daughter will contribute to our being better prepared. Last spring, the healthcare system in New York was put to the test. Now winter is coming, and we will be tested again. This is the world we live in, but I'm lucky to have Bobbi and Matt. And I wouldn't trade my credentials for anything. That talk of retiring? Of becoming a small-town doctor? Forget it. I love helping people. I love my emergency room; I love the action. I love the Bronx. I love my job.

Dan Koeppel's Afterword

While my cousin Rob was driving Bobbi to medical school, my family was planning a camping trip, and on Labor Day 2020, we drove to Maine's Acadia National Park. (I invited Rob and learned, for the first time, that camping was not something he'd ever contemplated or wanted to contemplate doing.) As we headed north, my wife, Kalee, and I noticed everyone who was wearing a mask—and everyone who wasn't. Either way, it was a statement. But beyond the politics, those visual declarations of belief and attitude were a reminder that Covid-19 wasn't over. I knew that. My two little kids would start school in the middle of the month, and we'd been told that they would have just two abbreviated days in person each week. That left families like mine, and hundreds of thousands of others in similar situations across the country, scrambling for childcare.

For anyone who thinks this pandemic is a fabrication or something less than this book makes it out to be, I refer to the families and loved ones of the dead, the dying, even the recovered. And then there's the collateral damage that Rob said would emerge when the pandemic eased: the non-Covid medical cases that, because of fear and neglect, had become more serious than they otherwise would have been.

"We're going to see death and sicknesses from advanced cancers, advanced coronary disease, lots of other stuff," Rob told me. All through the spring, the hidden sick—those corollary illnesses—were something we talked about.

ON MAY 1, I WAS STRICKEN WITH A HIGH FEVER AND STOM-ach pains. Like everyone, I thought it was Covid-19. I called Rob, and he advised me to head to my local emergency room, just two blocks from our apartment in downtown Portland. I walked into an unusually calm setting. There was a screening tent, and everybody was masked and gowned, but Northern Light Mercy Hospital isn't Montefiore. There was hardly a patient in sight. The doctors swabbed me, took my temperature, drew blood samples. Then, because I was in abdominal distress, they sent me down the hall for a CAT scan.

An hour later, I was released. Whatever was wrong with me, it wasn't Covid. My tests revealed no obvious issue.

And so I continued working on this book with Rob, interviewing him and his colleagues, fact-checking, doing all the things co-authors do. Because the deadline was so tight, we had enlisted the help of a freelance editor, Julie Shigekuni, who worked alongside me.

And then everything changed.

In early June, I went with my wife and kids to her family's cabin on an island in the middle of Lake Winnipesaukee, in central New Hampshire. Like Rob's Rockaway Beach, this place, Welch Island, brings me deep happiness. It was where I first met my future in-laws, more than fifteen years ago. It was Fourth of July weekend, and as we stepped onto the dock, my wife's father immediately handed me a beer and a lobster. (I was sold.) I've spent so many lazy summer days there, sitting by the water, reading or writing. I've spent nights in that unheated cabin, shivering as magnificent summer thunderstorms rolled through. But this time, my ability to turn off my worries was stopped short by a medical concern. I was urinating blood. Not a little. And it was disturbingly dark.

Of course, I called Rob, and he reassured me. It was probably nothing. Maybe prostate inflammation. At my age, that was more than possible, and I already had a medical history of urological problems. But I was also alarmed by what I found when I googled "blood in urine": It could be a sign of bladder cancer.

I made an appointment with my urologist to check it out. A few days later, he took urine samples and sent them to a lab. He also examined me with a scope, but there was so much blood, he couldn't get a good view. On June 20, I got a call.

"Your urine test," my doctor said in a relaxed voice, "shows cancer cells." But there was a quick qualification. "There are lots of false positives with this test," he said. "I think it's likely you don't have cancer."

I got further reassurance from Rob and even, in the midst of interviewing him, from John Gallagher. All said I likely had nothing to worry about, and all were right: It was *likely* I had nothing to worry about.

Even so, there was a problem. Because Covid-19 had led to so many delayed procedures, the confirming test, where the doctor would put me under general anesthesia and look for signs of cancer with a cystoscope (a rigid tool that probes the bladder), was not available for six weeks. It seemed too long to wait.

And so Rob did for me what he has done for so many patients: He made the wheels turn. Within hours, he'd secured an appointment for me at Montefiore. All I had to do was get down there, and a urologist he trusted—one who'd treated his own father-in-law for bladder cancer—would perform the procedure in early July.

I felt a little abashed about the strings being pulled, and I was acutely aware how lucky I was to have a cousin who isn't just a doctor but such a caring and connected one. I was comforted by the fact that I knew, at this point, that Rob does this for everybody.

And so, on July 2, 2020, I stepped into a urologist's office just down the street from Montefiore in the Bronx. It was early in the morning. The waiting room was empty, and some of the seats were taped off to maintain the proper distance between patients. The doctor told me he'd never closed his office, not even at the height of the pandemic, precisely because of cases like mine.

"We'll have a look with a flexible cystoscope," he said. "Depending on what we find, we'll do a rigid cystoscopy, and maybe a biopsy." Being inspected like that, whether you're male or female, is not fun. But it took all of five seconds of mild discomfort for the preliminary answer to arrive.

"You've got cancer," the doctor said. And he explained that although most bladder cancers are very manageable, even curable, mine was more challenging. My tumor, about the size of a walnut, was nested in a hidden pocket called a diverticulum. It would be hard to get at. It couldn't be completely removed from the inside, nor could it be treated with less invasive immune therapies, like most bladder cancers.

"You've got stage III," he said, referring to the numeric rating system given to malignancies, with stage IV being the worst. "We're going to need to put you under general anesthesia. We'll biopsy the tumor and try to remove what we can."

Two hours later, I was in the emergency room of Montefiore, getting the same treatment I've described—and witnessed—as hundreds of other patients: a painful swab; blood drawn; temperature taken. While I waited, Deb White and I talked about her father; Sean, the PCT, told me about his body-bag-carrying technique. Angelo Baccellieri told me what vitamins and supplements I should consider. Then I was wheeled into an elevator and whisked away, high above the Covid Zone.

My room had a gorgeous view of the Manhattan skyline. It was a sunny day, and I felt safe and cared for, but I knew that eleven stories below me, though the pace had slowed, patients with Covid-19 were still coming in every day, and some of them were dying.

There was no chance my tumor could be fully removed during this procedure. Instead, as much as possible would be cut out, with pieces sent off to pathology. It was all happening so fast, but I'd still have to wait to find out what kind of cancer it was and what to do about it.

The news wasn't as good as I'd have liked. I had a high-grade—that means aggressive—tumor, and I'd need to start chemotherapy immediately to try to shrink it as much as possible. After that, I'd need surgery, and there was a chance my entire bladder would have to be removed. Moreover, bladder cancer is one that frequently recurs. Even if all my treatments were successful, there was a 30 percent chance the cancer would come back, and as my oncologist told me, "If it comes back, there's very little that can be done."

When I told my wife all this over the phone, my voice

cracked. I tried to hold it together while I spoke to my boys, who were ten and five at the time. I told them I loved them, and when I hung up, I heard a soft sobbing. I couldn't see my roommate—his bed was behind a curtain—but I asked him if he was okay.

"Man," he said, "I'm sorry. I just lost it when you spoke to your kids."

My roommate, too, had just been diagnosed with cancer. His children were grown, and they weren't able to come and see him. Over the next two days, as I recovered, Brian and I talked about everything *but* our futures. One thing we agreed on: Both Covid and cancer are evil. We didn't have to argue or decide which was worse. Both felt very close at hand. Rob and Bobbi visited me a couple of times, including once with a giant sandwich from one of the Italian delis near Montefiore. I have to admit that I kind of marveled at the one tiny wisp of good luck in all this: I'd been given the chance to view the hospital I was helping to write a book about from the perspective of an actual patient rather than just a journalist.

But once I got home, the not-so-good began to outweigh everything else. Covid was subsiding, but I was getting sicker and sicker. While I started chemotherapy, I spent most days trying to write or read as much as I could between bouts of nausea, deep fatigue, and cognitive impairment, all known side effects of the treatment I was receiving.

Going from writing about my cousin to having my life saved by him was not what I had planned. My cancer was so fast-growing that the tumor was now apple-sized. The speed with which it expanded showed that Rob's intervention, and the way he got me in to see the urologist so quickly, made a huge difference. My summer of treatment meant that our collaborator, Julie, had to step up and take a much larger role, working to complete the book while I spent most days in that foggy, weakened, nearly broken state, struggling with my weekly four-hour, multidrug infusions. I read Aleksandr Solzhenitsyn's *Cancer Ward* on the days I felt too weak to write, and though the Soviet-era novel is more than sixty years old, his description of one of the side effects of cancer therapy still rings true: "a heaviness much greater than the weight of his body . . . so heavy he thought he'd never be able to get up on his feet again." In short, it sucked.

The good news is that I've responded well to chemo. As of this writing, my tumor has shrunk to the size of an acorn. That bodes well for my surgery, and it puts me closer to the 70 percent for whom bladder cancer doesn't recur.

In some ways, having cancer is easier than writing a book. The treatment is algorithmic, based on evidence. Writing a book—when it is done right—is based more on feeling than formula.

Becoming a Covid statistic—even a corollary statistic, being among those who have some malady whose treatment might have been subject to a life-threatening delay—was not my intention. But I think it helped the book, in a way. Experience is valuable. Nobody knows more about being sick than a sick person, and though I didn't get sick because of Covid-19, I did risk getting sicker because of the pandemic.

But I'm lucky. Not just to have Rob and Julie, but to have my family. I have a wife who is a brilliant editor and has done more than her fair share of caregiving. I have two young children who know that I am going through a medical drama. They sweetly offer to help by bringing me treats or just cuddling with me. But at the same time, they've seen my lack of energy, my chemo-based confusion, my physical upset. At Acadia, while they hiked and swam and went on boat rides and ate lobster rolls with their mom, I sat at the campsite and tried to focus. Mostly, I just rested. My five-year-old asked me, "Daddy, why are you in bed all the time?" The question broke my heart. I'm supposed to be playing with my boys, teaching them to ride their bikes, reading books to them, leading them on adventures. I don't want to be "Sick Dad," but my son understands, at least on some level, because this has been a year of illness for the world. He's reminded every time he has to put on a mask to go ride his scooter; every time he grimaces at the smell of hand sanitizer; every time he has to attend a birthday party via a computer screen.

So now this book is complete. But my treatment isn't, and neither is the pandemic. What I share with victims of Covid is uncertainty. But I also feel a sense of confidence. I have seen brave doctors save lives. I have seen brave families lose loved ones and go on living.

With gratitude to Rob and Julie, I hope the next few years will be not just about pressing onward, not just about overcoming a medical challenge, and not just about returning to something normal, but also about discovering something new. Because in the end, this story is not about death but about life. It's about how, from hardship, we grow as human beings. We honor those we've lost. We acknowledge those who've helped us. And we remember, most of all, to live for the moment, which is something far more than just surviving.

Acknowledgments

In 1996, I shook hands with Dr. E. John Gallagher, my mentor, second father, and friend. We agreed I'd work in the emergency department at Montefiore Medical Center in the Bronx. I promised him five years. Twenty-five years later, though recruited by other facilities many times, I'm still here. I have always been proud to say I work at Montefiore, but never more so than during the Covid-19 pandemic. Yes, we were caught by surprise like the rest of the world, but we quickly recovered and did whatever was necessary, without regard for cost, to provide the best care to the people of the Bronx.

I would not be a doctor today without the guidance and support of my father, Leon "Duke" Meyer. Having suffered immeasurable tragedies in his life, he has somehow been able to overcome all of them to encourage me to keep fighting through adversity. The doctor I am is also in large part a result of the influence of the late Dr. Richard Koeppel, my co-author's father and a longtime ER physician. To this day, Richard remains one of the greatest diagnosticians I've ever known. The third great influencer in my medical career has been Dr. Gallagher, who I believe is one of the world's finest clinicians, and who is with me, figuratively, every time I see a patient. These three guiding lights in my life taught me always to do whatever is in the best interest of the patient, to be a patient advocate at all costs.

This book would not have been possible were it not for a simple text from my cousin Dan Koeppel. A prolific and brilliant writer and journalist, as well as a husband and a father of two amazing boys, Dan, in the face of tremendous adversity, took a deep dive into everything that is the Bronx, Montefiore, the people in this book, and, of course, virology. We share great-grandparents, Max and Minna Porper, and the power of those shared genes is truly fascinating. We've had casual contact over the past five decades—Dan spent most of that time living in California, while I was on the East Coast—but after sharing one giant sandwich bought at Ann Clairs Italian deli at the corner of Morris Park Avenue and Williamsbridge Road in the Bronx, I realized we were one. Dan's ability to get inside my head is at times frightening. Indeed, this book and the process of writing it have been something of a catharsis and form of therapy for me, with Dan being the best therapist I could ever ask for.

Dan headed the editorial team, but I also want to acknowledge the huge contribution made by Julie Shigekuni, who did not have the benefit of shared DNA and fifty years of family history, and yet somehow managed to find ways to get at the deep connective tissue between anecdotes and moments that might otherwise have been weakened by standing alone. Laurie Liss at Sterling Lord Literistic patiently explained how the book business works and found the best possible home for this project at Crown, with editors Libby Burton and Gillian Blake.

I'd also like to thank a loosely knit group of friends who, in our ongoing text exchanges over the years, are referred to as "the boys"—Pete Kennelly, Charles Balancia, and Tom Tropea. They have always provided shoulders to lean on, brutal honesty, inspiration, and a good measure of wiseass sarcasm, all of which I appreciate equally, all of which got me through the Covid crisis. Similar gratitude to Scott Pearlman, whose office has always been a place of refuge, thanks to his obsession with great coffee: 42 grams of ground beans, 700 milliliters of water at 205 degrees. But while we certainly appreciated the barista in Scott, once Covid started, his office became a place to be normal again. We figured out a way to doff our PPE without wasting it and even managed to drink the coffee in a manner that did not put us at risk of transmitting the virus that we knew nothing about.

Angelo Cannarella and Ed Pfleging, along with Tom, made me feel normal again. There were times when I felt incredibly isolated, and you guys made me know that I wasn't alone.

I owe a huge debt to everyone who is connected to "90," our shorthand for the address of our building at Montefiore: Rob Fusco, constantly calling me a hero, knowing how uncomfortable that made me. Sal, Vinny, Maddie, Nicole, Mark, and so many others who cooked for me, made sure I put on the appropriate mask in order to protect myself, or sent a text just to say hi. You all made an enormous difference.

Erica Hezi was my kids' guidance counselor in high school—the same profession both my parents pursued—and she extended that guidance to me. You've been encouraging me to write a book for a long time, so here it is.

Richard Goldstein, who kept me nourished when I had little to no desire to eat. I will never eat barbecue anywhere else again. Joe and Leslie Montanile, whose daily check-ins and baking were a perfect way to close Richard's meals. David Cohen and Gregg Navins, who kept my spirits up with constant invitations to go for walks and bike rides or to come over for dinner. Anthony Venditto, who embodies the Bronx to me: Your inspirational texts meant so much. Eileen and Bill, who constantly reminded me that it was more than okay—it was essential—to hold somebody's hand every single day. Gary Rosen, who has been my moral and ethical barometer, pointing me in the right direction whenever I felt lost. Craig and Marilyn, whose home was the destination on so many walks: You knew when to listen and let me cry.

To all those who sent me bottles of mescal: You got me through this. Ditto for Scot Nicol of Ibis Cycles, who helped me with a major and sanity-saving bike upgrade during the heart of the crisis.

Matthew, your unparalleled sense of pragmatism and calm was so refreshing. I leaned on you more than you realized for an escape from the world.

Bobbi, you have been after me to write my story for years. I am only sorry that it took a pandemic and a text from Dan to make it happen. Your clinical acumen for one so young is humbling. You always knew when I was just feeling anxious and not really sick. That cannot be taught. As you embark on your medical career, do not lose that intuition. Do not get caught up in the minutiae of medicine. Continue to use your gut and instincts.

Janet, I truly do not know how you do what you do. Our relationship seems very one-sided. If you were afraid for my safety and life, you never once showed me that. You knew I needed you to be strong for our family and me. You never once allowed me, even for a second, to pity myself, and you did everything right. You were willing to get sick, which is the ultimate sacrifice. And please keep the bags packed, we'll be traveling again soon.

Finally, and most important, there was no way I could have survived going to work during this time were it not for all of the efforts of every single one of my colleagues: the nurses, patient care technicians, respiratory therapists, physician's assistants, nurse practitioners, housekeepers, registrars, and facilities workers. We were all in it together. I'm especially grateful to my physician colleagues for rising to the occasion, leading by example, and making it impossible for all of us to do anything but overcome the adversity that was everywhere. Your open and honest dialogue in our meetings, your candor about your pain and suffering, made me realize I was not alone. And to Dr. Deb White and Dr. Jesse Baer: Thank you for working tirelessly to put the rest of us in a position to succeed.

Rob Meyer, Hartsdale, New York, October 2020

FIRST, THERE'S MY WIFE, KALEE THOMPSON. WHILE I WORKED on this book, simultaneously undergoing chemotherapy and numerous medical procedures, she somehow managed to help me find the time I needed to rest, write, and recuperate, while juggling her full-time job, her own book project, and two rambunctious young boys, all while school was closed and the usual distractions we rely on to keep our children busy were out of service. I want Kalee to know that I understand how difficult this was for her.

I'd also like to thank Julie Shigekuni, whose role in this project was maddeningly shifting in definition. My agent, Laurie Liss, turned what began as a vague text message into a solid proposal and then a completed book deal, in a matter of days. At Crown, both my editors—Libby Burton and Gillian Blake—helped guide this book into the right place over the six months it took us to complete the writing. If you think about how the pandemic changed, how the world changed, during the spring and summer of 2020, you'll get a sense of how exactly *what* this book would be became a moving target. Libby and Gillian kept us pointed in the right direction even as the target shifted.

The first emergency room doctor I'd like to thank is my late father, Dr. Richard Koeppel. This book provided the missing piece of a puzzle for me: why he never encouraged me to follow him in his profession (even when I took and passed my first-responder course). I think my dad knew that being a writer was what I was meant to be—it's one of the things he wanted to become before choosing a more traditional path—and he also had Rob to fill that role. I'm grateful that my father took Rob under his wing, encouraging him instead to continue the family business.

I also want to thank all of the physicians and staff at Montefiore, who were patient with us as we interviewed, reinterviewed, and fact-checked, sometimes forcing them to repeat stories that were heartbreaking and difficult for them to recount.

Finally, I'd like to acknowledge my cousin and coauthor, Dr. Rob Meyer. This book allowed me to get much closer to him, to really know him and his family in a way that I hadn't before. (How could a guy who loves mountain biking, a sport I also adore, hate camping so much?) It was a joy to have him and Janet meet my boys; it was a joy to see Bobbi and Matt as young adults, both of them eager and ready to make the world a better place. I'm so grateful for the hard work Rob put into completing this undertaking, and the side benefit of growing closer to him turned out not to be secondary at all: For me, it has been the best thing about this project.

Dan Koeppel, Portland, Maine, October 2020

Notes

Foreword

xviii **Almost one thousand died:** Rafi Kabarriti, N. Patrik Brodin, Maxim I. Maron, et al., "Association of Race and Ethnicity with Comorbidities and Survival Among Patients with COVID-19 at an Urban Medical Center in New York," *JAMA Network Open,* September 25, 2020, https://jamanetwork.com/journals/jama networkopen/fullarticle/2770960.

Part I: March 2020

4 **By early March:** Centers for Disease Control and Prevention, "CDC Announces Additional COVID-19 Infections," news release, March 3, 2020, https://www.cdc.gov/media/releases/ 2020/s-0303-Additional-COVID-19-infections.html.

5 **On March 5:** https://www.nytimes.com/interactive/2020/us/ new-york-coronavirus-cases.html.

5 **More than a thousand a week:** https://www.nytimes.com/ interactive/2020/us/new-york-coronavirus-cases.html.

Chapter One

17   **The data on survival rates:** Stacey Burling, "If You Need a Ventilator for COVID-19, Odds Are 50-50 You'll Survive," *The Philadelphia Inquirer,* April 21, 2020, https://medicalxpress.com/news/2020-04-ventilator-covid-odds-youll.html; Judith Graham, "'No Intubation': Seniors Fearful of COVID-19 Are Changing Their Living Wills," Kaiser Health News, May 12, 2020, https://khn.org/news/no-intubation-seniors-fearful-of-covid-19-are-changing-their-living-wills/.

Chapter Two

33   **There are sixty-two counties:** https://www.health.ny.gov/statistics/chac/indicators/.

Chapter Three

41   **According to one study I've read:** Audrey Moukarzel, Pierre Michelet, Anne-Claire Durand, et al., "Burnout Syndrome Among Emergency Department Staff: Prevalence and Associated Factors," *BioMed Research International,* January 21, 2019, https://www.hindawi.com/journals/bmri/2019/6462472/.

46   **We're beginning to understand:** Andrew E. Budson, "The Hidden Long-Term Cognitive Effects of COVID-19," Harvard Health Blog, October 8, 2020, https://www.health.harvard.edu/blog/the-hidden-long-term-cognitive-effects-of-covid-2020100821133.

Part II: April 2020

107   **Covid deaths continue to climb:** https://www.usatoday.com/story/news/politics/2020/04/05/surgeon-general-jerome-adams-coronavirus-rivals-pearl-harbor-9-11/2950230001/.

Chapter Seven

125   **the emergency department's "general":** https://www.nytimes.com/2020/04/11/opinion/sunday/coronavirus-hospitals-bronx.html.

Chapter Eleven

166   **As many as 20 percent:** A. Mukhopadhyay, B. C. Tai, K. C. See, et al., "Risk Factors for Hospital and Long-Term Mortality of Critically Ill Elderly Patients Admitted to an Intensive Care Unit," *BioMed Research International,* December 16, 2014, https://www.hindawi.com/journals/bmri/2014/960575/.

Chapter Thirteen

184   **The refrigerated trucks, each of which held:** W. J. Hennigan, " 'We Do This for the Living': Inside New York's Citywide Effort to Bury Its Dead," *Time,* May 21, 2020, https://time.com/5839056/new-york-city-burials-coronavirus/.

187   **"no effort without error and shortcoming":** Erin McCarthy, "Roosevelt's 'The Man in the Arena,'" Mental Floss, April 23, 2015, https://www.mentalfloss.com/article/63389/roosevelts-man-arena.

Sources, Names, and Methods

This book was constructed from the direct recollections of Rob Meyer, as conveyed through conversations, emails, diary entries, text messages, voicemails, and voice memos. The events described here are based on our remembrances of actual situations, supplemented by in-person and virtual interviews. To maintain the privacy of the patients described, key details, including age, gender, ethnicity, profession, place of residence, and more, have been changed. In addition, we have omitted some of the names of medical personnel, especially when they were not authorized to speak by their employers. Interviews were conducted by Dan Koeppel, Rob Meyer, and Julie Shigekuni. Those conversations were then compiled and transcribed by Dan Koeppel, Julie Shigekuni, and (in most cases) professional transcribers. Nearly all of our interviews, when technology permitted, were recorded. All recordings were made with the permission of the interview subjects, who knew they were speaking on the record for a book. When recording was not possible, interviews were transcribed as text.

We have done our best to ensure that the thoughts and memories of our interview subjects and other sources are accurate and reflect their heroic efforts to save lives and, in some cases, survive themselves. Most sources were given the chance to review their statements and make corrections to them, but if any omissions or errors of fact remain, whether in the medical accounts or in the stories of patients, they are our responsibility and not that of our sources.

The general time lines and specific chronologies of events are based on popular news accounts. Covid-19 numbers were gathered from the World Health Organization, the U.S. Centers for Disease Control and Prevention, and the Johns Hopkins Coronavirus Resource Center. Additional sources included *The New York Times, The Boston Globe, The Washington Post,* and *The New England Journal of Medicine.*

Although most nonmedical folks still use the term "emergency room," physicians and medical professionals prefer "emergency department." This expression stands apart from other appellations that are often—but inaccurately—used interchangeably, such as "trauma center" and "urgent care." We generally use the term "emergency room" in this book because we believe that's what readers understand,

and we apologize in advance to those who feel that doing so gives short shrift to the modern specialty of emergency medicine. Similarly, we mention numerous medical facilities. Anyone who has followed American healthcare in recent years understands that mergers, consolidations, and legal changes have led to facility names being altered, sometimes repeatedly. We use the current names of the facilities, but in some cases those names may not line up with previous usage. We apologize in advance for any confusion this might cause.

Robert Meyer and Dan Koeppel

ABOUT THE AUTHORS

ROBERT MEYER, MD, has been an emergency room doctor for more than twenty-five years, spending most of his career at Montefiore Medical Center in the Bronx, whose emergency rooms are New York City's most visited and one of the nation's five busiest. He is an associate professor of emergency medicine at the Albert Einstein College of Medicine. He grew up in Queens, New York, and lives in Hartsdale, New York, with his wife, Janet. He has two grown children, one in medical school and the other in college.

DAN KOEPPEL is a former executive editor at *The New York Times*'s Wirecutter. He has written for national publications, including *Wired, Outside, National Geographic,* and *The Atlantic,* and won a James Beard Award for his food writing. Koeppel is also the recipient of a National Geographic Explorers Grant. His screenwriting credits include *Star Trek: The Next Generation,* and he is the author of *Banana: The Fate of the Fruit That Changed the World*. His writing has been anthologized three times in The Best American Series. He grew up in Queens, New York, and lives in Portland, Maine, with his wife, writer Kalee Thompson, and their two young boys.

Twitter: @soulbarn